LYNNETTE KHALFANI

ZERO DEBT

for COLLEGE GRADS

From **Student Loans** to **Financial Freedom**

KAPLAN

PUBLISHING

New York

Editorial Director: Jennifer Farthing
Acquistion Editor: Shannon Berning
Production Editor: Julio Espin
Production Artist: Ivelisse Robles Marrero
Cover Designer: Kathleen Lynch, Rod Hernandez

Published by Kaplan Publishing,
a division of Kaplan, Inc.

Printed in the United States of America

May 2007
07 08 09   10 9 8 7 6 5 4 3 2 1

ISBN 13: 978-1-4277-5464-6
ISBN 10: 1-4277-5464-0

Contents

Part Two: Pay Off Student Loans

INTRODUCTION:

THE STUDENT LOAN DILEMMA

Two out of three college graduates in America leave school with student loan debt—chances are that you are one of the graduates struggling with this burden. This is an enormous change from a generation ago when less than a third of college grads had to borrow money to achieve their dreams of obtaining a higher education.

Today, the typical graduate of a four-year college or university owes nearly $20,000 in student loans, more than double the median student loan debt of $9,250 just a decade ago. Unfortunately, for scores of adults, the hefty student loans they received while in school have now dashed their hopes for a financially secure future.

The problem, in a nutshell, is that skyrocketing school costs, declines in federal aid, and sagging wages have all combined to make student loan debt a tremendous burden for tens of millions of people in the United States. From fresh-out-of-school 20-somethings to 45-year-old workers who earned their degrees two decades ago, more and more college graduates are struggling under the weight of gigantic student loans.

Alarmingly, this situation could get worse before it gets better, especially if college costs continue to escalate each year. According to the College Board, the total annual cost of attending a public, four-year college or university in the 2006-07 school year—including tuition, fees, room and board charges—was $12,796, up 35% over the past five years. For private schools, the annual price tag to get a college education in 2006-07 was a whopping $30,367.

THE FALLOUT FROM THE STUDENT LOAN CRISIS

If you or someone you know has educational loans, you're probably all too familiar with the dire consequences of the burgeoning student loan crisis. Massive college debt impacts virtually every aspect of an individual's life, from his or her career choices to a person's plans for getting married or having a baby. Many financially strapped former students—armed with degrees they thought were supposed to land them high-paying jobs—are forced to go back home to live with Mom and Dad, swelling the ranks of the so-called "Boomerang Generation" who can't afford to live on their own.

This trend is apparent in many ways: For starters, 24 years is the average age that children now leave their parents' home, according to Demos, a New York-based public policy and advocacy group.

Yet every day, at campuses all across this nation, growing numbers of students are literally mortgaging their financial futures. To keep up with the surge in higher educations costs, students are accepting loans that in many cases will require a lifetime to repay. If you've been a recipient of federal student loans—or those increasingly popular private loans—you're certainly not alone.

According to the most recent data available from the College Board, about 8.5 million postsecondary students and parents received a total of $69 billion in loans through the federal government in 2005-06. On top of that, undergraduate and graduate students borrowed an unprecedented $17.3 billion from banks and other private lenders. Getting that money was fairly easy.

But repaying that debt is an entirely different story. In a survey commissioned by the Project on Student Debt, fully 66% of those polled described repaying student loans as either "very hard" or "fairly hard." If college grads could readily pay back these loans, perhaps there would be less concern over mounting borrowing costs. But there is overwhelming evidence that repayment of student debts is a major challenge for college graduates of all ages, incomes, majors, and ethnic backgrounds. Huge student loan debt also disproportionately burdens members of minority and low-income communities.

It wasn't supposed to be this way—and it doesn't have to be.

Lessons from Financially Liberated College Grads

I realize that the situation may seem bleak—if not downright impossible—for many of you, particularly those of you earning modest salaries and staring at a huge stack of student loan bills. But trust me when I say that it is possible to dig yourself out from your debts. I know because I've done it successfully.

Many of you have read my previous *New York Times* bestseller called *Zero Debt: The Ultimate Guide to Financial Freedom*. I wrote that book after I rid myself of $100,000 in credit card debt. Like many of you, I got my first credit card when I was a freshman in college. That marked the beginning of years of financial mismanagement on my part because—despite all the things I learned as an undergrad at the University of California, Irvine—nobody taught me a thing about how to budget, manage debt wisely, or be financially responsible with credit cards in my youth. I'm guessing your college experience was pretty much the same.

After I earned my Bachelor's degree in English from UC Irvine, I went on to obtain a Master's degree in journalism from the University of Southern California. By the time I was done with all my schooling, I'd racked up nearly $40,000 in student loans. Now I'm the first to admit that I've made my fair share of financial mistakes over the years. But happily, I managed those student loans well, and steadily paid them down year after year.

Still, I don't want you to just take my experience as proof that you can do the same thing. Throughout *Zero Debt for College Grads*, I'll

Myths Vs. Facts About Student Loans

Myth: I'm not currently in school or unemployed, so I won't qualify for a deferment or forbearance that would postpone my student loan payments.

Fact: Enrollment in classes and being out of work are merely two circumstances that can qualify you for a deferment. But Sallie Mae, the nation's largest holder of student loans, permits people in 18 categories to secure deferments. Working mothers of pre-school age children; women who are pregnant or caring for newborns/newly adopted kids; volunteers at tax-exempt organizations; those with high debt-to-income ratios; and people earning less than the minimum wage can all seek loan deferments.

Myth: If I can't pay these student loans off, I'll just file for bankruptcy protection to get rid of this debt.

Fact: Student loans generally can't be discharged in bankruptcy proceedings, except in very, very rare cases.

Myth: I didn't graduate from an expensive school, a private university, or a college where the cost of living is high, so my student loan debt probably is lower than other graduates.

Fact: A number of factors influence loan indebtedness. So merely attending a public school, or one with low-cost tuition is not a predictor of how much student loan debt you'll have.

Myth: Even though I don't make lots of money right now, at some point I will earn enough income due to my college degree to pay off my student loans.

share with you the insights I've gleaned from student loan experts, strategies from other graduates who've successfully paid off college debts, and even secrets from people who've managed to snag the Holy Grail for indentured grads: a federally approved discharge or cancellation of all student loans. Wouldn't it be nice to have all your college debts suddenly, almost magically, disappear? Well, it's rare, but it is doable—if you qualify, if you're tremendously persistent, and if you know some critical do's and don'ts.

Fact: Although most ex-students will have the wherewithal to eventually pay off their higher education debts, some college grads will—by choice or by circumstance—have low-paying jobs that will not enable them to fully retire their student loan debt. Also, some graduates will face chronic conditions, such as persistent unemployment, medical illness, or other hardships making it difficult, if not impossible, to completely repay student loans. Fortunately, alternatives exist for these individuals, as will be explained throughout *Zero Debt for College Grads*.

Myth: I'm so broke that even if my lender, the government, or a bill collector tried to squeeze some money out of me to repay my student loans, they couldn't get anything.
Fact: The Department of Education has sweeping powers to see to it that you pay back your loans. Your wages could be garnished, your income tax checks can be seized, and if you don't pay up by the time you retire, even your social security payments can be levied.

Myth: I got my student loans so many years ago, that even if I default they can't come after me.
Fact: There is no statute of limitations on educational loans, meaning you could be blind, 100 years old, and laying in a hospital bed, and a lender or creditor could still hunt you down and try to force you to repay a decades-old college debt.

■ ■ ■

Even if your student loans exceed your annual salary—which is, unfortunately, a common phenomenon these days—you can knock down those debts and start to regain control of your financial life. *Zero Debt for College Grads* will show you how to do just that. But to rid yourself of those pesky student loans, you need to first dispense with a number of misconceptions and myths you may have been hanging onto about college debt.

As you can see from the "Myth vs. Facts" on the previous page, there is no shortage of misconceptions when it comes to student loans. I don't want you to buy into any of these myths because they can stop you from making progress in your battle to knock out your college debts. Some of these wrong-headed myths may also put you in a state of inertia, or perhaps cause you to take actions that are not in your best financial interest—so it's important to set the record straight and separate fact from fiction.

Is a College Education Worth the Price Tag?

While you were in school, piling on loan after loan, you no doubt thought it would be worth it because everybody kept telling you that people with Bachelors or graduate and professional degrees stand to earn substantially greater incomes than those without degrees. In fact, that is very true. According to U.S. Census Bureau statistics, college grads earn about 62% more annually than do high school graduates; that works out to a $1 million earnings gap over a lifetime. If you're like me, you're thinking: "Great, but how is that going to help me pay these enormous student loans and other bills *today*?!"

Here's where I come in as your own personal Money Coach. *Zero Debt for College Grads* will not only tell graduates like you how to tackle your student loans, this book will also help you eliminate credit card debt and enjoy the stress-free financial lifestyle that all former college students want to lead.

It's one thing for a university sophomore or junior to share living quarters with multiple roommates just to cut expenses, to go Dutch on dates, and live off Ramen noodles. But in the "real world," after you've left your college campus, you'll likely want the privacy and comfort of your own place, a dating life that's not completely hampered by a barebones budget, and the ability to enjoy nice dinners out every now and then (i.e., at restaurants that *don't* have golden arches).

Like every transition in life, graduation comes with a whole new set of circumstances. Those making the initial foray into living "on their

own" often find it tough to deal with their new-found status as suppos-
edly independent, responsible adults. It's at this point in life that college
grads must grapple with a host of societal expectations that are suddenly thrust upon them—especially the notion that, just because they're
toting a degree, college grads are somehow miraculously capable of being fiscally responsible for themselves. Not even the top schools in the
country prepare students for this huge economic challenge.

Why Current Students, College Grads, and Parents Need This Book

Zero Debt for College Grads is the financial blueprint needed by anyone trying to juggle student loans, credit card debt, and any number
of bills associated with being on one's own. This book will help the
young and old alike—everyone who has taken on student loans and
is now trying to manage or repay those debts.

If you're still in school, but worried about how you'll ever get
ahead once you graduate with big loans, consider this book your
secret weapon for preventing financial problems down the road. If
you're a 20-something recent graduate facing a range of "start-up"
costs—like the money you have to fork over for your own apartment,
or the cash you need to spend on a new wardrobe as you get started
in your career—you need *Zero Debt for College Grads* as your roadmap
for a financially independent life.

If you're in your 30s, 40s, or 50s—perhaps many years out of
school but still grappling with student loans, mounting credit card
bills, and everything from childcare costs to car payments—then you
also need *Zero Debt for College Grads* to get schooled on the multitude
of financial options available to you.

And what about the parents of college students, those of you who
may have tapped the equity in your homes, exhausted your personal
savings, and also taken out school loans to finance your child's education? Don't worry: There is plenty of advice that will help you,
too. Despite the title, *Zero Debts for College Grads* isn't just for former

students who, after years of arduous work, have taken home a hard-earned degree. This book is also for the parents who love them—and who generously helped foot their sons' and daughters' college bills along the way. In fact, 41% of parents plan to pay the full tab for their children's education, according to a survey from Alliance Bernstein Investments. That kind of benevolence is admirable; but you shouldn't have to sacrifice your retirement in the process.

HOW TO USE THIS BOOK

Zero Debt for College Grads contains three sections focusing on juggling your current monthly bills, paying off your student loans, and managing your credit. The meat of this book—well over half of it, in fact—is devoted to helping you solve the student loan dilemma. But before you can do that, you need to learn some basic personal finance rules and money management techniques. That information is contained in the book's first three chapters.

In the second section of *Zero Debt for College Grads,* I'll walk you through everything you need to know about managing and ultimately getting rid of those student loans once and for all. You'll find out whether you're eligible for a loan cancellation. I'll explain how student loans impact your credit rating, offer guidance on loan consolidation, and reveal how you can quickly get past-due loans out of default. You'll also discover the range of repayment plans available, no matter what your circumstances. Did you know you can pay as little as $5 a month for certain student loans? After you gain a thorough understanding of how it is that you'll beat your student loan debt, I'll share with you my insider secrets for wiping out credit card debt and establishing a great credit rating.

If having Zero Debt, and being liberated from those onerous student loans is high on your list of goals, read on. It's well past time you got started on the pathway to financial freedom!

■ Part One

Manage Today's Bills Wisely

1

PERSONAL FINANCE 101

Smart Rules about Budgeting, Credit, and Debt

In college we all learn lots of things that, hopefully, will help us throughout life. Many of us learn how to work in teams, how to better communicate with others, and how to take new information and apply it in various ways. Lots of college grads also learn technical skills such as how to perform surgery, argue a court case, or write computer programs. Unfortunately, the one thing we don't learn in school is how to manage our bills wisely.

When I look back at my days as an undergrad and graduate student, I can't help but wish that in addition to Psych 101, biology, and an assortment of humanities and journalism courses, someone would have taught me the basics of money management. In this chapter, my goal is to give you a crash course in money management. How else are you going to pay off your student loans, get a wardrobe for the new job, and start your savings? Let's call it Personal Finance 101. The lessons I'll share will prove just as valuable to you, I hope, as many others you learned while toiling to get that hard-earned degree.

FIVE CRITICAL MONEY-MANAGEMENT LESSONS YOU DIDN'T LEARN IN SCHOOL

To keep on top of your bills, and learn to better manage your personal finances, there are a slew of routine measures you can take and strategies you can use to get ahead financially. But college grads of all ages would do particularly well if they understood the following lessons—and then applied these lessons in their everyday lives. With that said, here are five critical money-management lessons you didn't learn in school, but should have:

1. Everything always costs more than you think it will.
2. Even millionaires have a budget.
3. Your credit standing is as important as your degree.
4. Credit cards and student loans are not free money.
5. Saving now saves problems later.

As I elaborate on each of these lessons, you will begin to understand how you can put the wisdom of these principles into practice. Later in this chapter, you will come face to face with the reality of your financial situation by creating your own budget.

1. Everything Always Costs More Than You Think It Will

I used to think that only young college grads made the mistake of underestimating how much it costs to live in the real world. After working as a money coach, however, and talking to countless individuals about their monthly finances, I've since discovered that people of all ages, incomes, and education levels fall into this trap. It's very common for me to talk with 30- and 40-year-old professionals about the "average costs" of their living expenses, and have them give me figures that I know are way off the mark.

For example, a 35-year-old trying to save for retirement might think that having $1 million in the bank 20 years from now will be sufficient during her golden years. The truth is, she may live to be 90 or even 95. If she wants to have an early retirement, at age 55, she needs to make sure she has enough savings to last 40 years in retirement—and $1 million probably won't cut it.

Beyond the dream of a comfortable retirement, everybody in this country wants something—from the mundane to the extraordinary. More often than not, there's a price tag attached to the things we want to buy, do, have, or achieve.

For example, getting an education is a costly endeavor, as you well know. It's not just about performing academically or being willing to spend years in school studying and taking tests. You must also come up with the financing for a higher education—these days, anywhere from $20,000 to $30,000 or more for a four-year degree.

Think about virtually any goal you'd like to accomplish—whether it's buying a home, traveling around the world, taking a photography class, or just being able to paint on the beach whenever you'd like. All of these things come at a price. Unfortunately, most people vastly underestimate the true cost of reaching their goals. And even when people put an accurate price tag on the cost of having or experiencing the things that they want, they overestimate their own financial resources and their ability to pay for those items.

Never overestimate your income or expect to land a high-paying job that's far above the national average. Along those same lines, you also should avoid a common mistake made by many recent college grads. Simply put: don't equate your gross income with your ability to pay various bills. Just because you're making $40,000 a year doesn't mean you'll be bringing home $40,000 annually. And it certainly doesn't mean you should go out and buy a $40,000 car!

The truth of the matter is that if you're grossing $40,000, you're in the 25 percent tax bracket, and so your net income—that is, your salary after federal, state, and Social Security taxes—will be about $30,000. Translation: every two weeks your paycheck will be roughly $1,154; every month you'll be taking home $2,308. In some areas,

It's Not What You Make—It's What You Keep!		
Gross Annual Income	$40,000	$53,333
Minus Annual Taxes (25%)	–$10,000	–$13,333
Net Annual Income	$30,000	$40,000
Net Monthly Income	$2,308	$3,077

that $2,308 can go a long way, but in many parts of the country, you'll be pinched for cash—especially if you have a family.

Notice that your $40,000 income produces an after-tax, or net, monthly salary of $2,308. But you'd have to actually earn a gross salary of $53,333 in order to net $40,000 annually, which leaves you with a take-home pay of $3,077 each month.

With these numbers in mind, take a look at this classic example of what happens with the typical college graduate who is fresh out of school. Assume this college grad is named Nadine Naïve. Nadine thinks that because she landed a $40,000 a year job, she'll be able handle her bills with no problem.

What Nadine hasn't counted on, though, is that the apartment in the city in which she wants to live costs $1,000 a month—twice as much as she'd planned on spending for housing. Nadine's new job as a marketing specialist requires her to meet with clients and take part in high-level meetings with senior executives. So needless to say, Nadine wants to "look the part." There goes $300 a month on clothes to get the wardrobe started. She has to get to work, of course, so Nadine has a used vehicle, with a modest $200 a month payment.

Because Nadine is now on her own and no longer living with her parents, car insurance is a new expense she also must tackle. That's a $150 a month hit to her wallet. Throw in another $100 a month for gas, tolls, and commuting expenses, along with maintenance costs for automobile oil changes and the like. Did I mention that Nadine has student loans? Those are $150 a month. Credit card bills from debts she ran up in school are another $200 each month. As tight as things are, we don't think Nadine will starve herself, so we'll assume she's eating some food; groceries and eating out costs $300 a month.

You may have noticed by now that Nadine Naïve is actually spending more than she makes. On these "basics" alone, she's spending $2,400 a month (and she's only bringing home $2,308 each month)! We haven't even talked about how Nadine will furnish her apartment or pay for utilities like gas, water, and electric service, her cell phone bill, Internet service, or cable TV—let alone indulge in a few luxuries like trips to the nail and hair salon.

Basic Budget for Nadine Naïve

Monthly Net Income	+$2,308
Rent	−$1,000
Clothing	−$300
Car Payment	−$200
Insurance	−$150
Gas & Auto Maintenance	−$100
Student Loans	−$150
Credit Cards	−$200
Food	−$300
Total (At End of Month)	−$92

The lesson here is that almost everyone underestimates the true cost of living—not to mention setting aside money to achieve future-oriented goals. Without a true handle on your actual or expected living costs—a budget—you'll always be spending more than you make and you'll never get ahead financially, which leads to the next lesson.

2. Even Millionaires Have a Budget

If you're operating without a normal monthly budget, that's a huge mistake. In fact, the lack of a budget is a big part of the reason that the average American now has nearly $10,000 in consumer debt, most of which is personal credit card debt. Of course, many people have mortgages, auto loans, student loans, and other consumer debt. But it's possible that you can have tons of bills and still exist in a state of denial about your finances. I know because I did it for a very long time before waking up and deciding to fix my debt problem once and for all.

For a lot of people, *budget* is a four-letter word because they often picture a budget as something that restricts them—something that says: you can't have this, you can't buy that, or you can't do this. Well, that is the wrong way to look at a budget. A budget is really a part of your personal prosperity plan. It's the financial blueprint you'll use to help you get where you want to go in life. Without a budget—without a clear sense of exactly how many dollars are coming in the door and how many dollars are really going out each month—you're doomed to constantly live paycheck to paycheck.

A budget helps you manage your cash flow so that you can more readily achieve your personal and financial goals, including paying off those student loans. Unfortunately, statistics show that 65 percent of all people don't operate with a basic monthly budget. That's a real shame because a lack of a budget explains, in part, why so many people don't know where the money goes.

Have you ever been in a situation where you thought "Gosh! I just got paid last week and now I'm broke" or "I don't know what happened to my money; it seems to have vanished just as quickly as I got it"? The simplest way to identify and fix the problem is to come up with a realistic budget to operate from on a regular basis.

Believe it or not, even millionaires have budgets. In my previous book, *The Money Coach's Guide to Your First Million,* I talk about my own transformation, and how I went from debt to wealth. But I also highlight tips from many other people—millionaires and other financial experts. And all of them agree that having a budget as the basis for your spending plan is a smart way to exercise control over your dollars—instead of letting your money control you.

No matter how you configure your budget, to have a proper, successful budget, you need only conform to two rules:

1. Your spending cannot exceed your income. Sounds basic, I know, but most people don't stick to this one little rule. In fact, the average household in the United States spends $1.22 for every dollar that it earns, according to a study from Northwestern Mutual.

2. Your budget must include a savings component. Without some level of savings worked into your budget, you'll always be behind the proverbial eight ball. Later in this chapter, I'll give you some tips on how to create and successfully use a realistic budget—one you can live with and one that isn't overly restrictive.

Maybe you're thinking, "I don't have any money, so why budget?" You still need to write out your expenses so you can understand how much you need to earn or whether you need to cut back on certain areas.

3. Your Credit Standing Is as Important as Your Degree

No doubt you tracked your grades carefully throughout school. Now you have an even more important report card to pay attention to.

Every one of you reading this book should know what's in your credit report, and even further, what your current FICO credit scores are. To get your credit report from any of the big three credit reporting bureaus—TransUnion, Equifax, or Experian—you can order your credit file by telephone, online, or using good old snail mail. I tend to like things faster, so I'm more apt to do things over the Internet and get information instantly. You're also entitled to get one free copy of your credit report from the credit bureaus by logging onto *www.annualcreditreport.com.*

Your credit report will show you what debts you have outstanding and whom you owe. Most importantly, your credit report details the status of all your accounts: listing them as paid or unpaid, charged off or current, and so forth. It will give you the addresses and often the phone numbers for your creditors should you need to contact them.

Your credit file will also indicate whether any negative information is contained about you in public records—things like court judgments, bankruptcies, and state and federal tax liens against you or your property.

To get your FICO score, you have to go to the company that originated it. FICO stands for Fair Isaac Corporation. It is the Minneapolis-based company that develops credit scores for tens of millions of people in this country. FICO scores range from 300 to 850. The higher your score, the better a credit risk you are. A high FICO score also shows that you've done an excellent job of managing credit and debt—something that, as I will explain shortly, can help you save or earn more than $1 million over your lifetime. Find out your FICO score by visiting *www.myfico.com*.

While there are multiple types of credit scores available, FICO scores are seen as the gold standard when it comes to credit scores. About 90 percent of all the top banks in this country use FICO scores to determine whether or not to extend you credit and at what interest rate; this includes mortgage companies, credit card issuers, auto lenders, and other financial entities. Having a great credit file—and particularly having a high FICO credit score, is often better than having cash in the bank. In fact, having a great FICO score can be just as important to you as that degree you spent so many years pursuing. Countless numbers of college grads ruin their credit while in school by accepting too many credit cards, maxing out their accounts, paying bills late, or, even worse, not paying at all...and then find that they can't even get jobs in their field because of poor credit. Don't make this mistake. You must jealously guard your credit at all times—and not just think about credit when you're in the process of applying for a loan of some sort.

Most college students don't know that their FICO credit score, and their entire credit standing, affects so many aspects of their lives—or will in the future after they graduate. When you are trying to get a job, did you know that an employer can legally pull your credit report and look at your FICO score and determine whether or not to extend a job offer to you? On your existing job, your current employer can also pull your credit report, look at your FICO score, and determine whether or not to give you a promotion. When you are in the market for auto insurance, did you know that your auto insurance rates are determined, in part, by your credit score? The same thing is true of life insurance. Your life insurance rates are set, in part, based on your credit standing and your credit score. Those with great credit will be offered better, more affordable life insurance rates compared with those with poor credit, who will be forced to pay higher insurance premiums

Always guard your credit rating. Don't let your future career options be limited because you mishandled your credit and debt. I have heard of cases where job offers have been put on the table (in writing no less—with formal salary packages, benefits, and a slew of perks), only to have those offers rescinded once the company has done its review and found a candidate's credit to be poor. It may not sound fair but it certainly is legal. So these are some of the ways in which your credit clearly impacts you in a very big and real way—and it goes far beyond your ability to get a loan.

Your ability to earn a livelihood plays a very crucial role in your financial success in life. You've probably heard of the statistics from the U.S. Census Bureau that point out that the average college graduate earns 62 percent more than does the average high school graduate. Over a lifetime that translates into about a million-dollar earnings gap. So clearly you want to get those good, high-paying jobs. But you won't be able to if poor credit hampers you.

And increasingly, more and more companies are doing routine credit checks as a condition of you coming to work for them. It doesn't matter what kind of job you're seeking. In some companies, everyone must pass a credit check—from the janitor to the CEO. That's the case, for instance, with HSBC Bank. I once did a workshop for about 120 bank employees in Chicago, teaching them about the importance of maintaining great credit and about the ways in which your credit standing can either help you get ahead in the workforce or hold you back. So don't think, "Well, I'm not going to work for a bank" or "I won't be handling any customer funds." The trends in place suggest that routine credit checks will become the norm in all industries, regardless of what type of job you're seeking. So this alone is one reason why it's important to maintain an excellent credit profile.

The trouble, however, comes in when we are not taught about financial literacy. Many of us have our first experience with credit cards in while we are in college, at the age of 18, 19, or 20 years old. Unfortunately, that's the time most of us learn all the wrong things about credit—which takes us to the next lesson.

4. Credit Cards and Student Loans Are Not Free Money

Millions of college students blow it big time when it comes to taking on credit card debt and student loans. I don't know how it happens. Actually, I do know at least part of the cycle with credit cards. You walk on campus and a credit card marketer is there, saying something like: "Hey, want a free T-shirt?" All the student hears, pretty much, is the word *free*.

Sure, you know that you've got to pay back the bank for all those charges you make. But for most students, that's a distant concern. They're enchanted by the idea that they can (in their own minds) get something free today, simply by slapping down a piece of plastic at a department store or retailer of their choice. But credit cards are anything but free—and neither, of course, are student loans.

In fact, using the word *credit* for people in college is a particularly egregious misnomer. The word *credit* often has a positive connotation for college students. You've all heard the expression, "I give him credit for doing this or that." And what about college students who love to get "extra credit" from professors? As you can see, in most contexts, the word *credit* gets used positively among students, and that's the time at which many people are most unsophisticated, vulnerable, and likely to get tripped up by using credit the wrong way. But it might help you to think about a credit card as what it really is: an IOU card.

None of this is to suggest that credit is inherently a bad thing or that you should not have credit at all. For many people, having credit allows them to function in society in a seamless way, and to use credit as a convenient method of payment. Credit cards enable us to do everything from shop online to rent automobiles. So the idea isn't to say, "I'm never going to use credit cards again," especially if you have had a financial problem. The challenge is to determine: "How can I manage my credit cards well and what should I be doing to make sure that I am a smart and savvy consumer in order to leverage my credit standing in a way that gives me the most benefits?"

Not only are credit cards and student loans not free money, they are borrowed funds that can actually be quite costly if not properly managed or if allowed to linger on year after year. With credit cards, you're really getting an up-front loan to pay for various purchases, so in this manner, credit card debt and student loans aren't that different. They're both fundamentally loans.

And for the privilege of receiving that loan, you'll pay dearly in most cases. The typical credit card has an interest rate of about 15 percent, according to Cardweb.com. That means for every $100 you charge, you'll pay an extra $15 on top if you take a year to pay the bill. If you miss a credit card payment, you could find yourself in the unfortunate predicament of having a "default" interest rate, which now runs as high as 35 percent on some cards. While most federal student loans offer single-digit interest rates at less than 9 percent, if you stretch out your student loan payments (as most college grads do), you can wind up paying two to three times your original student loan amount because of interest charges alone!

With that credit card, you'll also face a slew of charges, such as annual fees, cash-advance fees, finance charges on the outstanding part of your bill, late payments, and over-the-limit penalties.

Don't ever accept a credit card offer or student loan without a very good idea about how you will repay it and how long that repayment will take. Too often students simply think, "Oh well, I'll worry about that bill later." That's not smart financial planning, and it's the easy way to financial ruin. One reason for that is you'll probably take on more student loans and more credit card debt than you anticipate. Remember the first lesson, "Everything always costs more than you think it will"? Well, the same thing is true with your educational costs too.

Why would higher education cost more than you estimate? A big reason is that many of you mistakenly think you'll finish school in just four years. Those days are long gone. Students take an average of 6.2 years to complete their degrees in public universities, and 5.3 years to graduate from a private school, according to the Conference Board. For those who aren't conscientious about the debts they take on, this means additional student loans and more credit card debt racked up along the way.

5. Saving Now Saves Problems Later

Everyone wants to *have* more money, but not everyone wants to save more money. Yet the two go hand in hand. Many of you have read my previous book, *Zero Debt: The Ultimate Guide to Financial Freedom*, in which I talk about getting out of debt and saving more money, as well as learning how to manage your own personal budget. It's critically important that you learn how to budget and set aside money on a regular basis, because otherwise you're destined to constantly be broke and in debt. And who wants that?

Developing the discipline necessary to save money in the here and now—despite all the other things competing for your cash—may be one of the single biggest factors in determining whether or not you'll live a wealthy, financially prosperous life. Without saving, you'll always be in the hole. You'll always be forced to pay for big-ticket items with credit. You'll miss out on the opportunity to let time work on your side, and you'll forgo the benefit of compounded interest. Do you realize that saving just a little bit of money now—and I'm talking $10 a week if that's all you can spare—can actually reap huge financial benefits down the road? Ideally, you'll want to build up a three-month cash cushion. This means that you should have a

How Much to Save?

Try to save 10 percent of your take-home pay each month. If you can save 10 percent of your gross salary, that's even better. However, just because you may not be able to afford to save at the 10 percent level, that doesn't mean you should forgo saving altogether. Set aside whatever amount of money you can afford on a regularly basis (weekly, biweekly, or monthly) until you amass three months' worth of expenses.

Example of a Savings Target:
Monthly Bills: $3,000
Savings Goal: $9,000

You won't accumulate a three-month cash cushion overnight. But if you sock away money from every paycheck, little by little your savings account will grow.

savings safety net that is equal to three times your normal monthly expenses.

Saving money regularly allows you to build up a cash cushion that protects you against the inevitable blows that we all face in life—things like getting a pink slip from your employer or dealing with a car with mechanical problems. Imagine how much stress and financial trouble you'd be in if you were totally reliant upon that job, or completely dependent upon that car to get to work? If you were out of a job, how long could you last without that steady paycheck?

Many of you have problems making ends meet right now, even with that paycheck coming in every two weeks. So if you didn't work for, say, a month or two—or possibly longer, if you were trying to find a new job—what would it mean for you and your family? How would you live, survive, and pay your ongoing bills if you didn't have some savings set aside?

Trust me when I say that it's in your long-term best interests to put away some money for unexpected events in the future. Call it a rainy-day fund or whatever you'd like. But take the time to establish a "hands-off" account that you don't touch. The goal is to only put money into that account, not drain it for any number of reasons. You only take money out of that savings account for true emergencies, or to pay for things that you've budgeted, planned, and saved up to purchase.

I have three children, including an infant daughter. With my older two, who are now nine and seven years old, I teach them all the time that they have choices with their money. I gave them a nifty piggy bank, called the Money Savvy Pig, from the Money Savvy Generation (*www.moneysavvygeneration.com*). The Money Savvy Pig is a 21st-century piggy bank, with four slots in it instead of just one. It comes with stickers and labels that say "Save," "Spend," "Invest," and "Donate." Again, the idea is to teach kids that they have choices about how they use their money. But that's a message that a lot of us adults should remember too!

COMMON BUDGET-WRECKERS

With a little positive financial planning, you can make sure that these common budget-wreckers don't happen to you.

- Forgotten bills. These typically are those things that you have to pay quarterly, or maybe on an annual basis. Examples include auto insurance, membership fees, and other sporadic bills.
- Emergencies. Protect yourself against unexpected events with a little preventive medicine. Don't find yourself in a situation where your car engine seizes up just because you failed to put oil in the car. Or don't allow your whole roof to cave in just because you didn't take care of a small leak right away. Take the basic precautionary steps that are necessary to prevent small-scale dilemmas from become large-scale financial nightmares.

- The 20 percent rule. To maintain a realistic budget, implement something that I call the 20 percent rule. In a nutshell, this rule says that whatever the bottom-line number you come up with in terms of your monthly expenses, add 20 percent to it. So if you tell me that your bills are $2,500 a month, I'm automatically thinking they're really 20 percent more, or $3,000 monthly. The reason for this strategy is that many people underestimate their bills. Also, the extra 20 percent allows you to build a cushion in your budget. I don't want your budget to be so tight that every single penny must be accounted for or your whole budget is thrown out of whack. That's too restrictive. If you find that you really didn't spend that 20 percent extra, but you did budget for it, simply put it into your savings or use it to pay down debts.

CREATE YOUR OWN BUDGET

Here's my simple two-step process for creating a basic budget. It's fast, easy, and anyone can do it.

Step 1: Itemize ALL of Your Expenses

Create a list of everything you spend money on—whether those expenditures are weekly, monthly, or yearly. Use different categories to group all your expenses. Examples of common budget categories include:

- Child care
- Credit card payments
- Educational costs or student loans
- Entertainment
- Food
- Housing
- Insurance

- Miscellaneous
- Savings
- Transportation
- Utilities

Obviously, some of these categories may not apply to you. Use whatever is relevant or add additional categories that describe your own spending. Be thorough! Don't forget about annual memberships, magazine subscriptions, books, or money spent on gifts for birthdays, graduations, holidays, and special occasions. Your list can be written or entered on a computer spreadsheet.

Step 2: Adjust to Avoid Budget-Wreckers

If your expenses exceed your income, you'll have to cut back on areas that aren't necessities. Stop going out to dinner. Say goodbye (temporarily at least) to that premium cable TV package you have. Forgo shopping trips to the mall.

After you quit making luxury purchases or spending money on things that aren't absolute necessities, if your expenses still surpass your income, you'll have to make additional adjustments to your budget—this time slimming down on even those "necessities." You should also adjust your budget to avoid the common budget-wreckers I described above. Don't ever think "There's no place else I can cut my budget!" I hear this lament all the time, and invariably I'm able to show people places in their budget where they do have some flexibility—if they choose to make deeper cuts.

While you're adjusting your budget to match up your spending and income, the goal is to first get your expenses down so that they're less than your take-home income. Then you want to create enough cash flow so that you have some money left over at the end of the month—and you're not merely living paycheck to paycheck without getting ahead. To jumpstart your efforts, fill out the basic budget on the next page.

My Basic Budget—Monthly Net Income: $

Item	Cost
Child Care	$
Credit Card Payments	$
Educational Costs/Student Loans	$
Entertainment	$
Food	$
Housing	$
Insurance	$
Miscellaneous	$
Savings	$
Transportation	$
Utilities	$
Total (At End of Month)	$

STICK TO YOUR BUDGET

Hopefully, you can get your budget to the point where you have a positive cash flow. But sometimes you may find that while your income is sufficient to cover all your bills, you nevertheless find it difficult to save money or stick to your budget. There are many reasons why people do not stick to their budgets.

- Some people never truly itemize their expenses. Consequently, their spending exceeds their income.
- Others exclude key categories from their budget. Two key categories in particular that I find people tend to omit from their budget are savings and goals. If you want to get ahead, if you want to actually save money, a category for "savings" has to be included in your personal budget. You might also want to achieve certain personal or financial goals, like getting out of debt, starting a business, or purchasing an investment property. To reach those goals, you have to be willing to consistently set aside money in your budget each month to finance those goals.
- Many people create budgets that are excessively frugal. Nobody can stick to an overly restrictive budget month in and month out. It is

kind of like the dieter who wants to lose 10 pounds or 20 pounds. The person might say, "I am never going to eat another piece of chocolate cake" or "I am never going to touch another bag of potato chips." Well, how realistic is that? For most people it is very unrealistic. You do not want to deprive yourself when you create your budget. So do not create one that is excessively frugal.

- Some people blow their budgets because they do poor planning or no planning whatsoever.

BOOST YOUR FINANCIAL IQ

Let's turn now to ways in which you can make yourself a smarter, savvier person from a financial standpoint. What you're doing right now—creating a budget—is certainly helping. I also applaud anyone who takes the time to read books, personal finance magazines, or newspapers that can teach you about money management. For further suggestions, please see the Resources at the end of the book. You can also take courses (even cheap ones at a community college or an adult education/continuing learning facility) that focus on personal finances.

It also pays to surround yourself with people who are doing better than you are financially. If you know people who are very well off financially, even better. Ask them for strategies they've used. Find out what they did—and didn't do—to achieve wealth. Don't be afraid to say flat out that you're trying to turn your financial life around, and that you're interested in discovering practical money-management strategies that work.

Change your mind-set from a purely consumer-driven mentality to one that is consumer savvy. In other words, don't just think about what you want or need to buy, think about the smartest ways to get what you need. Do you really have to purchase those books from the bookstore? Or is it possible to borrow them from the library? Should you buy those clothes right now—or wait until they go on sale? Can those groceries you need from the supermarket be purchased less expensively if you simply clipped a few coupons? The idea is to be conscious about your spending and financial habits. Don't merely turn over your hard-earned dollars to the first open hand. Be wise about when, how, and with whom you're spending your money.

Finally, make comparison shopping a normal and regular part of your life. Any time you buy something, always think: where can I get it cheaper, or is there a way to decrease the cost of this purchase? Let's say you're buying soda from the store. Instead of a 12-ounce can would it be better to buy a 2-liter bottle? When you're comparison shopping, the Internet is a great equalizer because you can find tons of information online and quickly get a sense of whether a product or service you're looking to buy is overpriced or a real bargain. Even offline, be on the lookout for ways in which you can exercise your mind—building your financial IQ every step of the way.

In the chapters that follow, you'll learn to cut your costs and find more money for your budget. After all, if you can find some extra money in places you may not have considered, or if you can shave your expenses on monthly items such as housing, clothing, transportation, and more, you'll create additional cash flow—and more quickly knock out those hefty student loans.

CHAPTER

2

CUT YOUR COSTS

*Save on Housing, Transportation,
Clothing, and More*

In 2007, I appeared on the *Tyra Banks Show*. The show's theme was "Living Large on Small Change" and it was my job to give two students—who were also guests of the show—some advice on how to live within a budget. These young women were 20 and 21 years old, but they'd been living off their parents—and living quite large I might add.

They dressed exclusively in designer clothes, they drove expensive cars, and they lived and partied like they were celebrities. Other students on their Florida college campus had taken to calling these young women Paris and Nicole—after Paris Hilton and Nicole Richie. And the young women had even adopted a moniker to describe themselves: HRP, which stands for "Hot, Rich, and Popular."

LIVING LARGE ON SMALL CHANGE

Imagine their surprise when I told them that they couldn't have their designer bags and $500 shoes, and that they'd have to rough it like true college students. It was a hoot when I took away their credit cards and cell phones and forced them to live on the typical budget of today's college student. Here's a snapshot of what that budget looks like.

According to Upromise.com, the average college student earns $7.50 an hour and works 25 hours a week. That translates into $187.50 a week. Even if a student worked full-time at 40 hours a week (which most don't, because they have classes, labs, papers to write, and more), that would only amount to a gross salary of $300 a week, or a measly $15,600 a year.

But, of course, everyone has to pay taxes. So let's assume federal, state, and local taxes will amount to 30 percent—meaning Uncle Sam will take $90 out of that $300 a week. What's left is a paltry $210 a week! If a 21-year-old is netting $210 a week, that would be $840 a month.

Here's a breakdown of how the money should be wisely spent, based on various categories of expenses:

Budget Item	Maximum Percentage	Dollar Amount
Rent/Housing	35	294
Car Payment	15	126
Food	15	126
Savings	10	84
Car Insurance	5	42
Utilities	5	42
Clothing	5	42
Entertainment	5	42
Miscellaneous	5	42
Total	100	840

These numbers may seem ridiculously low, but they reveal the types of costs college students must contend with. Obviously, not everyone sticks to the formula or guidelines above. Many will spend more or less on entertainment, others will devote considerably more to housing, and so on. But in terms of dollars, most college students are on a severely restricted budget.

It's generally not much different when you first graduate, so here are some smart ways in which college students and recent college grads can reduce their expenses in all of those areas. When you're on a limited income, every dollar you spend is precious, so you have to make sure those dollars count—whether they're for food, shelter, clothing, or other necessities, or for the occasional luxury you might find yourself indulging in or purchasing on a whim.

Save on Housing

Housing costs are a big chunk of everyone's budget, so it stands to reason that this may be the one area where you can significantly cut back on your expenses. In many cases it is possible, but for some of you, I warn you now: drastic steps may be necessary to slash your housing costs.

According to a Demos report titled *The High Cost of Putting a Roof over Your Head*, many recent college grads moving to start their careers face sticker shock at how much rent costs. Between 1995 and 2002, rents in virtually every large metropolitan area in the country rose dramatically. Demos reports that median rents in San Francisco surged 76 percent; rents in Boston mushroomed 62 percent; San Diego rents shot up by 54 percent, and even rents in Denver rose by 49 percent.

As a result, young adults now spend about 22 percent of their pretax income on rent, up from 17 percent in 1970. And more than a third of young adults spend more than 30 percent of their pretax income on rent.

Needless to say, it's also gotten a lot tougher for recent college grads to purchase a first home. In fact, in many parts of the country, college graduates are priced out of the market, and homeownership—a dream for many Americans—now seems more out of reach than ever.

To combat this economic dilemma, you have several options:

- Live in a less expensive city or a rural area where the cost of living isn't as pricey.

- Live with a roommate to cut costs and thereby decrease your monthly housing costs.
- Live in the city of your choice (even an expensive one) if you're willing to downsize your expectations. Maybe instead of a one-bedroom apartment, you have to settle for a studio. And maybe instead of living in the heart of a city's downtown area, you live in an outlying area that is more affordable. *Forbes* magazine provides an annual list of the best, most affordable places to live.

If you're still a student, seek out good housing deals specifically targeting students or former students. Some managers of off-campus apartment complexes offer good students discounted rent. For instance, students of California Polytechnic State University in San Luis Obispo, California, who live in the off-campus Valencia Apartments get a 5 percent discount on their lease if they earn a GPA between 3.0 and 3.5. If your GPA is 3.9 or higher, you qualify for a 10 percent discount.

The True Price of Your Car

To cut your transportation expenses, you'll need to first think carefully about your personal and professional needs and how critical it is for you to have reliable transportation. In some cities, like New York or Boston, having a car is unnecessary and will definitely set you back financially in ways that make it impractical, and often downright impossible, to own a car. In other places, like Los Angeles, you may feel like you desperately need some wheels to get around. If you do buy a car, or you already have one, here are some helpful cost-cutting suggestions to follow.

Be a smart car buyer. Do a thorough inspection and background check on any car you're considering buying. You can use a service called Car Facts (*www.carfacts.com*), which for a small fee will provide you with all the information you need to know about a car's history.

All you need to do is supply them with the car's vehicle identification number (VIN), which is the unique 17-character number that's found on the dashboard. Car Facts will instantly tell you everything you'd want to know about the car, such as whether there has been damage to it, what the odometer reading on it should say, how many owners the car has had, and whether it received regular service checkups.

As a savvy consumer, you certainly want to know whether someone's telling you the truth about taking good care of the car, or that it has low miles on it, or that it's never been in an accident. Car Facts collects data from government sources such as state departments of motor vehicles to help you confirm what the owner/seller of the car is telling you about the vehicle. When a car suffers major damage, the DMV labels the title of the car with names like "Flooded," "Salvage," or "Totaled," so you can avoid pitfalls like odometer fraud or buying a used car with flood damage. All of this can be useful information in negotiating a better price for the car.

Haggle over the price of any car you buy. Never simply pay the sticker price or asking price for a car, whether from a dealer or a private owner. Be prepared to negotiate for the best possible deal. Arm yourself with facts about the car's present value, how much it might depreciate in the future, and what comparable cars in similar condition are currently going for. You can find this information online through car-buying websites such as Edmunds.com or Kelly Blue Book (*www.kbb.com*).

If you're buying a car from an auto dealership, be firm about disregarding the sticker price on the car's window. Most people make the mistake of trying to bargain down from that price, which is also called the manufacturer's suggested retail price (MSRP). But *Consumer Reports* says you should first find out the dealer's invoice price-the cost they actually paid for the car—and then negotiate up from that number. Cars.com and MotorReports.com offer free information about how to calculate a dealer's invoice price, and how to get rid of bogus charges like "prep" fees or charges for VIN etching.

Remember to factor in all the costs of having a car. That means the car payment, the insurance, the costs of gas and maintenance, and any expenses you have to pay for storing the car or parking it in a garage at your residence or place of work. You'll also no doubt want to have the car cleaned every now and again. For some of you, the costs may outweigh the benefits, and you may decide that public transportation is a much better, much more cost-effective solution.

Seek out insurance discounts. You car insurance rate will also need some evaluation. It may have gone through the roof because you're no longer on your parents' policy. Also, you may not be getting that multicar discount if you move out of your parents' home and are no longer tied to their address. Additionally, insurers generally charge higher rates for younger, less-experienced drivers.

Nevertheless, you can get other auto insurance discounts that will help lower your overall car costs. For instance, some insurers will decrease your premiums if you have an alarm system or antitheft device, if you take a driver's safety course, or if you park your car in a garage at home instead of on the street. If you are still in school, getting good grades can help lower your rates too. Insurers see high grades as an indication that you are responsible. Therefore, most insurers offer a "good student discount" of 10 percent to 25 percent if you maintain at least a B average. Be sure to call your auto insurer to ask whether you qualify for any of these or other discounts.

When you purchase a car, realize that an automobile is a depreciating asset. As soon as you drive that car off the lot, it loses anywhere from 10 to 25 percent of its value, depending on the year, make, and model of that car.

Renegotiate your car payment. If you already have a car and your car payment is too high, you may be able to lower your payments through auto refinancing—and get a lower interest rate. Many people don't know that you can refinance your car loan just as you can refinance a mortgage. But a car refinancing is faster, simpler to do, and costs virtually nothing. Certainly there aren't any closing costs or points, like you might have with a mortgage. Most players in the auto refinancing business operate online.

The hands-down giant in this space is Capital One Auto Finance (*www.capitaloneauto.com*). If you refinance an auto loan with Capital One, it'll take just 15 minutes, and the average customer saves more than $1,300 over the life of their car loan.

So if your car has a high interest rate, check out a lender like Capital One to knock down your monthly car note and save yourself some big bucks. I once refinanced my auto loan with Capital One and saved more $100 a month on my car payments. Eloans.com also offers auto refinancing. If you do refinance your car, don't extend the life of your payments. If you only have three years left to pay off your car, refinance with a lender that lets you keep a three-year pay-off. Otherwise you'll stretch out your payments and wind up forking over additional money in interest charges. When you do save money with a refinancing, take your savings and pay off debt or use it to build your cash cushion.

Save on Food and Household Items

You can certainly add to your cash savings by eliminating wasteful spending or cutting back on things that only serve to take dollars out of your pocket.

Don't overindulge. How many days do you stop for coffee and donuts before you go to work? Many people spend about $5 a day on these items. Do you realize that five dollars a day during the work week translates into $100 a month, or $1,200 a year? Even those of you who don't hit the local Starbucks or Dunkin' Donuts on your way to work nevertheless make a junk food run to the vending machine every day at work. You're buying Snickers, chips, or soda and the like and spending $3 a day on junk food. If you cut that out, you could save 900 bucks in a year.

Makeover your medicine cabinet. You may love brand-name clothes and shoes, but when it comes to medicine, it definitely pays to ask your doctor or pharmacist for generic drugs. Request generics for any prescription you take. By law, generic drugs have the identical chemical makeup and active ingredients as brand-name medications—without the hefty price tag.

The average price of a brand-name prescription is about $100. Meanwhile, the typical generic drug costs just $30, a savings of 70 percent. So if you make one trip to the pharmacy each month, over the course of a year you'll save $840 just by using generic drugs instead of brand-name ones.

Stretch the stuff you buy and use at home. With a little effort, you can make a little go a long way. Here are some ideas to get you started.

- Stay away from pump toothpastes. They don't last as long as tubes. Also, you don't need as much toothpaste as most people think.
- Protect that soap. In the shower, keep your soap out of the water spray to make it last longer.
- Smell nice at a cheaper price. For deodorant, buy sticks or roll-ons. They last longer than aerosols, and they're better for the environment too.
- Get smart about mailing and postage expenses. Nix the monthly hassles of writing checks and scrambling for envelopes and stamps. Pay your bills online through your bank or an online service such as *www.mycheckfree.com* to save time and reduce your postage costs. If you pay ten bills a month electronically, you'll save about $50 a year on stamps. Not a whole lot, but every little bit counts. Also, send e-cards during the holidays and for birthdays. It completely eliminates the cost of postage and buying printed cards. Plus, it's more environmentally friendly.

Save Money by Breaking Bad Habits!

Certain habits are not good for you financially or healthwise. Cigarette prices top $4 a pack nationwide, excluding taxes charged by various states. If you've got a two-pack-a-day habit, that's costing you roughly $10 bucks a day on cigarettes alone! That's $280 dollars a month or $3,360 dollars a year. That is a large amount of money to fork over to the tobacco companies, and does not even include the medical costs associated with cigarette smoking in terms of your higher insurance premiums, lost time on the job, and so forth.

Think about your own situation and whether there are certain habits or activities that you engage in on a regular basis that you know are detrimental to you personally and financially. Cut those areas out of your life, and turn that money into savings.

Save on Utilities

You can save thousands of dollars just by making simple changes around the house. Here are some everyday energy tips:

- Get unplugged. Stop draining power and wasting money by unplugging appliances not in use—your toaster, blender, or coffee maker, for example. You'll cut your energy costs by 10 percent.
- Go light on light bulbs. Swap out high-watt bulbs for lower-wattage ones, or better yet, fluorescent light bulbs. These last ten times longer and use a quarter of the electricity. My honey and I did this recently, and our electricity bills dropped from $160 to $100 a month.
- Fill her up. Only run full loads of clothes in your washer/dryer. Ditto for your dishwasher.
- Take showers instead of baths. This single step can cut your hot water costs by up to 50 percent!

- Adjust your thermostat. Turn it up two degrees in the summer and down two degrees in the winter to shave up to 10 percent off your energy bill.

A Wardrobe on a Budget

Saving money on your clothes doesn't have to be a big hassle. It starts by getting the proper mind-set and resolving that you won't overspend on things you want and you will not spend without having shopped around for good deals. So many people fail to do this. They pay full price for products and services that they could have easily gotten for a lot less money. Nowhere is this more evident than when it comes to shopping for clothes.

How many times have you gone into a department store and bought something, and the woman at the cash register asked you if you had a store coupon? Were you kicking yourself for not simply clipping one out of that day's paper, or not bringing one that came in the mail? One minute of planning before you ran out the door to go shopping could have saved you 10 or 20 percent off your bill. I'm not suggesting you spend hours and hours coupon clipping. Who has time for that? What I am recommending, however, is that you get into the habit of trying to save yourself money in ways that are fast, easy, and sometimes downright fun. After all, it's exciting when you find a great deal or a bargain on something that you've seen for twice the price elsewhere. One of the best places to find rock-bottom prices on clothing is actually on the Internet.

Don't be so quick to buy the latest brand name clothes either. Who knows if that dress you're wearing is a designer label or a knock off from H&M anyway? I once bought a brown faux-leather purse from Target—one of those really oversized bags that are all the rage with celebs—and I paid a mere $19.99 for that purse. It is so cute and I can't tell you how many compliments I've gotten on that purse. Most people think it's an expensive designer bag!

By the way, when you're out shopping, avoid signing up for those store credit cards just to get a so-called savings of 10 or 20 percent. These cards not only carry very high interest rates, often around 20 percent, they can also lower your credit score. (See more tips on managing credit in the final chapters of this book.)

To avoid paying full retail price for your clothes you can do a number of things:

- Shop at outlets or discount stores.
- Wait until the item goes on sale.
- Bargain or try to haggle (in thrift shops, flea markets, some boutiques and specialty stores). A few strategies to help you haggle: Offer to pay cash instead of credit, point out any flaws in the clothing, or just make it look like you're ready to walk out the door.
- Shop online. Try *decadestwo.com* for vintage chic; *YOOX.com* for Italian designers; *StarWares.com* for celebrity duds; and *Bluefly.com, eBay.com,* and *Overstock.com* for a wide range of clothes.
- Shop sample sales and get even designer clothes at a fraction of the retail price. Check out sample sales after Fashion Week in New York and Los Angeles.
- Buy nice, classic clothes off season, when these pieces are cheaper
- Limit your purchases to a few key items that will go a long way: a black skirt, black pants, and black sweater for women, and a white button-down shirt and black slacks for men.
- Refuse to pay full price for anything!

Affordable Entertainment

Does your budget leave you without funds to have fun? Don't think that you're doomed to stay home every night or that you can't go out on dates.

Here are some ideas to get your creative juices flowing:

- Most museums have a day when you can enter for free.

B o n u s   T i p s

- Do your own home maintenance.
- Only go to your bank's ATMs.
- Bring lunch to work daily or a few days a week.
- Carpool.
- Use coupons (always or from time to time).
- Barter. Exchange your talents for something you need.

- Have a picnic in the park.
- Look for free events in your local paper: readings, lectures, and more.
- Enjoy the cultural and historical sites in your area; most are free or low-cost venues.
- Go to parties—all you need to bring is an inexpensive bottle of wine.
- Have dinner parties rather than going out to a restaurant.
- When you go to a club, get there early so you don't have to pay the cover charge.

MAKE SURE YOU'RE INSURED

Insurance is very important—in the long run, it can save you lots and lots of money.

As discussed previously in this chapter, car insurance is a must-have. But don't forget homeowner's insurance and health insurance.

If you are a homeowner, you no doubt have homeowner's insurance that you're paying on semiannual or annual basis. Some of you may have your insurance payments packaged into your monthly mortgage payment—this is known as PITI, where your payments cover principal, interest, taxes, and insurance. The average homeowner pays about $700 a year in insurance, according to industry estimates. A simple way to put some bucks back into your wallet is to reassess your insurance needs and make sure you're not overpaying for insurance, or overinsuring yourself needlessly.

Now I'm a big proponent of insurance—and I strongly believe that many Americans are woefully underinsured. That doesn't mean, however, that millions of people out there aren't paying too much for the insurance coverage they do have. Look at the areas of coverage you have, whether that's health insurance, car insurance, or homeowner's insurance. In all these cases, you can raise the deductibles on your insurance policies and save yourself money.

Increasing your insurance deductible to $1,000 from $500 can save you 25 to 30 percent off your policy—a big chunk of money considering that nationwide, the average cost of annual car insurance is about $880 dollars, and for homeowner's insurance it is about $700 dollars. So raising your deductibles in these areas alone can mean a quick $395 in your bank account.

Health insurance costs, as you likely know, are all over the place. And while it's very difficult to give accurate average costs, the one thing everyone does agree on is that health care costs are rising. So if you can stand to have a higher deductible policy, that might be something for you to consider as well because you will certainly save money on your health care costs, and that money can be readily put right back into your pocket.

For those of you who have Preferred Provider Organization (PPO) plans in terms of your health coverage, you might also consider switching to an HMO plan. With an HMO plan, you are confined to visiting a specific group of doctors so, in general, HMOs are more restrictive. But if you find that your doctor is already in a certain HMO network, you could switch without worrying about not being able to see your regular doctor, and save $200 or so each month.

All of these things will fatten your bank account and leave you more economically prosperous, money savvy, and feeling good that you are fast becoming financially free!

3

FATTEN YOUR BANK ACCOUNT

How to Find or Create Extra Money

Many of you reading this book would love to have some extra money, right? I don't know if you could use $1,000 extra each year, or $1,000 a month. But the cold, hard reality is that lots of us need some cold, hard cash!

Extra cash in your bank account could mean a lot of positive things for you. You could pay down debt with it—especially those student loans. You could jump-start your savings, particularly those of you who have been procrastinating about funding that cash cushion you know you need. You could certainly add to your retirement nest egg. You could do a laundry list of things with that extra money that would certainly be a benefit to you as long as you used the money in a positive way and didn't just blow it. So many times, unfortunately, we do just that.

We come into windfalls—big chunks of money beyond our normal weekly, monthly, or annual income—and, in short order, we've squandered the money. When I talk about windfalls, I am not talking about winning the lottery—you've got about a one in 25 million chance of hitting some multimillion dollar jackpot. I'm talking about more common windfalls that happen to people every day. It might be a tax-refund check, maybe an annual bonus on the job, or even some unexpected money that comes your way because of a lawsuit or a life insurance policy in which someone named you as a beneficiary. In your case, you may have received a nice chunk of money from your family upon graduation. All of these events, and others, constitute financial windfalls in our lives. And obviously, all these large cash infusions could be readily used to help you tackle college debt and other bills you are now juggling.

So where do you find extra money? In this chapter, I will suggest some ongoing ways in which you might reap your own personal wind-fall by generating additional cash and finding extra money that you may not have even known was due to you.

Unlike investing, where you have to put up money in order to generate a financial return, none of the ideas I'm about to share with you will require a single dollar out of your pocket. They all, however, will require your time. And if you're willing to spend a little time implementing these strategies, you'll find yourself flush with extra cash in no time flat.

SQUEEZE LOTS OF EXTRA MONEY OUT OF YOUR JOB

The logical place to look for more money is in your line of work. I've determined four ways you can start: negotiate a good package from a new employer, make sure the deduction on your W-4 is keep-ing money in your pocket, ask for a raise in an existing job, and take advantage of the benefits offered to you by your employer.

Negotiate a Strong Compensation Package

The best time to secure the most dollars from your employer is when you first get hired. That's the point at which you have lots of room to negotiate for a host of perks, including extra vacation time, annual bonuses, stock options, and more. When an employer really wants to bring you on board, you'll also have more leverage in getting a higher starting salary. You obviously want to bargain for the best possible cash compensation. But don't forget to look beyond just your paycheck.

Ask about benefits such as tuition reimbursement plans, and inquire about whether your boss would even pay off your student loans as part of an employment incentive contract to keep you as a loyal employee of the company. (Read more about getting your boss to pay your student loans Chapter 9.) Check out CareerJournal.com, from the *Wall Street Journal,* for lots of free tips and great information on negotiating a winning compensation package.

Get Your Money Up Front

Have you gotten a tax refund check in the past or do you anticipate getting one this year or in the future? Well anytime you get a big refund check from Uncle Sam all that really means is that you have given the government an interest-free loan. So adjust your withholdings at work. Do not get a refund check.

What you have to do is fill out a form called a W-4. You should also get IRS Publication 919, which walks you through the whole process of properly filling out a W-4. It's not overly complicated but this publication spells out in detail the ways in which you can adjust your W-4 at work. What you are going to do, in a nutshell, is increase the number of allowances that you claim on line five of your W-4 form. The goal is to decrease the withholding amount and ultimately receive a bigger paycheck. For those of you who usually get tax refunds, adjusting your W-4 at work will instantly put money in your pocket.

That extra money will immediately get funneled into your paycheck. So let's say you usually get a $2,400 refund, which is close to the average of what many people receive. Well, $2,400 dollars translates into $200 a month that you could be getting right now in your paycheck. If you get paid once every two weeks, expect to see an extra hundred bucks in each paycheck.

Clearly, when you consider ways to make or earn some extra money, put this strategy right at the top of your list.

Get That Well-Earned Raise

I know there are onerous bosses, but the truth of the matter is that if you want to put some extra money in your pocket you may have to deal with that boss yet, because one way to find yourself some extra money is to walk right into your boss's office and get yourself a raise.

Yes, even now in tough economic times, you can get a raise. I know some of you doubters are going to say, "Lynnette, there are layoffs taking place right now," or "My boss is a total tightwad," or "The company isn't doing so hot financially and they've told us no raises."

To all of those excuses I say: they don't matter.

There are two surefire strategies you can implement to make sure you get a raise—even during the worst economic conditions. First, you must constantly document your work accomplishments to demonstrate your performance and what you offer to the organization. In other words, do not just walk into to your boss and say, "I want a raise," or "I think deserve a raise." Your boss won't care that you've been doing good work, or that you've come to work every day on time. That's not good enough. That's a basic minimum level of expected performance.

You have to show—in numerical terms—how you benefit the organization. If you saved the company X number of dollars, if you created a new program that has generated a certain amount of income for the business, if you have been instrumental in training, if you have done hiring, if you have been a sales superstar, whatever it is that you have done, document that.

When you get performance appraisals, feedback, and e-mails from customers, peers, and your higher-ups, and they notice what you have done, keep a running log of all of those things. Those communications and feedback become part of your success story. That is what you are going to bring to the table, because ultimately the person with the most information is going to win when it comes to negotiating for a salary increase. Think of the dossier you create of all your accomplishments and various pats on the back for a job well done as your "Praise" folder—it's praise about the great work that you've done over the course of the year.

Second, always negotiate from a position of strength—not need or greed. Do not go complaining to your boss, "You know I just had a baby," or "My spouse and I just bought a new house and we've got tons of student loans and other bills to pay...blah, blah, blah." Most bosses don't care about your personal problems; they do not want to hear about your financial troubles or how many bills you have. So you need to negotiate in their language, with terms and information that is relevant to them. By telling you to negotiate from a position of strength, I'm suggesting that you show and quantify the value you bring to your organization. Demonstrate your accomplishments and make your case persuasively. Say: "This is where I have been extremely successful. This is where I have contributed. This is where I have been able to save money."

Be specific in what you want. Let's say the boss does turn you down. Assume that he or she won't give you a raise right now no matter how much you demonstrate your case, quantify your value, and negotiate from a position of strength. Here's what to do next to make sure you ultimately get that raise. Put the ball in your boss's corner. Not only are you going to be specific in saying "I want a raise," you are also going to make him or her justify why you don't merit one. You have to be artful here. But the idea is that you want to turn things around and say, "Well, I think I have made a very strong case as to why I deserve a raise.'"

Do not let your boss tell you about the cost of living adjustments, how nobody else got one, or how tough times are. Instead, put a blunt question to your boss. Ask "What do I need to do in order to get a

10 percent raise in one year's time?" Maybe you want that raise six months from now, or perhaps your boss will agree to revisit in the following quarter. But don't just ask for a raise. Ask for a specific raise, in percentage terms, and give it a time frame. Have your boss spell out what standards he or she would like to see you meet.

If there are performance issues to address, handle them. But your boss may say something like, "Well, I'd really like to see you meet X sales targets, complete this or that project, and brush up on your technical skills." Whatever the boss says, make sure you get an agreement in writing—even if it's just e-mail—so that you'll have the basis of an understanding surrounding the issue.

One easy way to do this is to merely go back to your desk, write your boss an e-mail saying thanks for meeting with me and here's my understanding, based on our conversation, of what you'd be looking for in order for me to earn a merit-based increase. Also note the agreed-upon time frame at which the two of you will revisit this topic. When you do go back, three months or six months later, if you've done all that your boss has asked—along with documentation of your accomplishments in your growing "Praise" folder—your boss will be hard-pressed to turn you down for that raise. When you meet his or her own criteria for performance goals, work measurements, and other targets, the boss will have little choice but to honor your justified request for that 10 percent raise, or else risk looking like a liar, or at least someone who doesn't keep his or her word. This is one way you really negotiate from a position of strength on the job.

Take Advantage of the Benefits Offered to You

For starters, if you contribute to your 401(k) plan at work, or a 403(b) plan if you work in the private sector or with a nonprofit, when you contribute to these employer-sponsored retirement savings plans, what you are effectively doing is reducing your taxable income. You save money for retirement but you also often get matching contributions from your employer.

So I do not care how mean or unfair your boss might be. Even if he doesn't like you personally and would never think to give you a raise, if your company has a 401(k) or 403(b) plan in which you're eligible to participate, there's nothing that tyrannical boss can do to stop you from contributing to that retirement plan and getting some money from the company in the form of a corporate match. That is free money on the table from your employer.

I tell people all the time: if you have a 401(k) plan at work or a 403(b) plan and you are not contributing, you are literally leaving dollars on the table. If you are getting a dollar-for-dollar match, that is a 100 percent return on your money guaranteed. You definitely cannot get that in the stock market or from any investment, so take advantage of it when it's offered.

For 2007, 2008, and 2009, the contribution limits for your 401(k) are $15,000, $15,500, and $16,000, respectively. Generally speaking, employers let you put up to 15 percent of your pay into a 401(k). If you are over 50, there is a so-called catch-up provision in the law that allows you to sock away another $5,000 dollars (an amount that rises to $5,500 in 2009).

So assume you make $50,000 annually and you put 10 percent of your pay, or $5,000, into your 401(k). If you employer matches even 50 cents on the dollar, they will put in half of your contribution, or $2,500 bucks.

TURN YOUR HOME OR APARTMENT INTO A GOLDMINE

For those of you at home, let's start by taking a look around your immediate vicinity. You might be sitting in a home that you own or reading on a sofa in an apartment. No matter where you reside, though, I hope you'll no longer think of your resting place as merely a roof over your head. In fact, the place where you live might turn into one of the biggest financial windfalls for you—a source you can immediately tap for some additional cash. Some of you are probably thinking that I'm talking about homeowner's tapping the equity in their homes. No, in most cases, I don't think it's prudent to arbitrarily tap the equity in your home, not even to pay off student loan debt.

Sell Stuff You Don't Use Anymore

Most of us have lots of stuff that, frankly, we just don't want, need, or even use any more. If you find that you have old computers at home that really are not being well utilized, or if you have clothing that doesn't fit or jewelry you don't wear anymore, take the time to get rid of some of that stuff in the most economically advantageous way possible. There are a few ways you could do this.

Sell unwanted goods directly. Simply go online to a site like eBay and list what you have for sale. But if the Internet sales route doesn't appeal to you, you could hold a garage sale. The average profit for a one-weekend garage sale is $600, according to Marilyn Pokorney, author of the e-book *200-Plus Secrets for a Successful Garage Sale*. Racking up $600 isn't bad for getting rid of things like old clothes, appliances, or small goods you no longer want, or other household items that would simply be put to better use by someone else.

Donate some of the things that you do not want for even bigger savings. Here's why: under federal law, the IRS says that you can deduct the fair market value of anything that you donate to an appropriate organization, in particular an accredited organization that is deemed a nonprofit. You'd be surprised at how most of us vastly underestimate the worth of the things that we donate. And that is to your financial detriment because you can get a big tax saving from your donations. For example, let's say you were selling a woman's designer pullover sweater at a garage sale. At what price would you be willing to let it go? And what about a little girl's dress that was in fair condition? Most times, these items sell for $5 (or less) at garage sales. But according to *ItsDeductible.com*, the fair market value for that sweater is $20, and $10 for that dress. You can see, therefore, how the savings can really add up if you're unloading a lot of clothes or other items you simply don't need.

Get a Roommate or Tenant

Some of you in very expensive parts of the country should definitely consider getting a roommate and/or renting a room in your house—or maybe even your basement, depending on your circumstances. You might say, "I don't have a house, I live in an apartment."

If you rent, you obviously first want to check your renter's agreement and find out if your contract forbids you from having a roommate. You don't want to create a nasty situation with your landlord by breaking the rules. But if your landlord is fine with it, then having an extra person in your house means having another individual to shoulder the cost of rent and utilities.

If you own your home, the decision is yours to make. You can figure out which room might be best to rent out, or see if a basement or attic could be readily converted into an acceptable (read: up to code!) living space. Taking on a tenant would provide you with a steady stream of cash month after month. In high-rent sections of the United States, this could be an especially attractive option because other people who want to be on their own may not be able to afford a whole apartment, but could swing paying for a room in your house.

If taking on a tenant full-time seems like too big a task, perhaps you could consider renting out your place on a temporary basis. For instance, you might rent out your place if you're away for the summer. You could lease your residence during the holidays or during a busy travel season. Many travelers from foreign countries often go through vacation exchange networks online to find people willing to rent out their homes or apartments. So if you're in an area of high demand, like Florida, New York, or California, take some time to investigate this option.

Believe it or not, many foreign visitors—because they have kids perhaps—would refer to be in a more residential neighborhood as opposed to staying in a hotel in a busy commercial district.

Itemize Your Deductions

One final way to use your house as a cash cow, without tapping any equity, is to get Uncle Sam to underwrite what is probably the biggest investment you have ever made in your life. Simply itemize your deductions.

Unfortunately, most people actually take the standard deduction on their tax returns. The IRS says that only about 35 percent of returns filed contained itemized deductions as opposed to the standard deduction. That is a big mistake, because in 2007 the standard deduction was $5,350 dollars for single individuals, $10,700 dollars for married couples, and $7,850 dollars for those designated as head of household. But if you were using your home to take every tax break and deduction you are entitled to, chances are your deductions would far exceed the standard rate if you itemize them.

For example, nationwide, the average person pays about $5,000 dollars in mortgage interest. (Some of you—on the East and West Coasts, in particular—may be saying: "$5,000! I pay that in a couple of months!" So your mortgage interest is obviously far in excess of the national average.) Also, property taxes on average nationwide are about $1,500 dollars. So the idea here is simple: do not miss out on the opportunity to take every deduction for which you are legally qualified with regard to your home. If you follow my advice, you will truly be leveraging your house and using the value of your house wisely.

Unfortunately, like I said, most people do not do it and Uncle Sam tells us that U.S. taxpayers lose about $1 billion in the aggregate as a result. Can you imagine? Millions of Americans collectively lose

$1 billion a year just because they have taken the standard deduction. And I know why some of you take that standard deduction. It's because you are rushing. You procrastinated, and you're filing your taxes at the last minute. Haven't we all seen the television with those long lines of people standing in line at the post office on April 15, trying to beat the midnight filing deadline?

I understand part of this insanity though. Tax forms are complicated and they take so much time. The IRS says it takes about 29 hours to fill out your taxes if you do it yourself. I turn that headache over to a CPA and call it a day! But no matter whether you do your own taxes or hire a professional, just be sure to use that house as a piggy bank (wisely, of course) whenever you can.

CASH IN ON THOSE FREEBIES
YOU'VE EARNED

Are you one of those people who spend like crazy on your credit cards, racking up tons of cash rewards, rebates, frequent flier miles, or other bonuses? Many people justify their spending (and in many cases, it's really overspending) by saying, "Well, I'm using this credit card because I get points for these purchases." Now is the time, then, to start cashing in some of those points.

Again, you can generate some additional money here without actually spending a single dollar. By the way, I am not suggesting that you go out and spend more on your cards. I am saying work with what you have. If you already have cash rebates, free amenities, and other perks that are due to you, go ahead and tap into those freebies—especially if you would've purchased those goods on your own.

When I last paid my American Express bill, I noticed that I'd accumulated over 36,000 points. My plan is to use those points for travel or for some type of reward where I would've spent cash. Many of these rebates and points won't amount to a heck of a lot if you try to turn them into dollars. But you can get the cash equivalent out of them by redeeming whatever points and perks you have coming to you, thereby saving yourself decent money.

Along these lines, you may also have gift cards you haven't used or mail-in rebates on purchases you've made. Go ahead and cash in on what you're owed!

IS "FREE" MONEY IN YOUR FUTURE?

Let's turn now to some quick sources of cash that you may not know about. First of all, do you know that 26 million Americans are currently the legal and rightful owners of unclaimed property in this country—to the tune of $100 billion or more?

Well, by various estimates, $100 billion is held by state governments alone. New York state, for example, is holding about $6 billion worth of unclaimed money. The federal government also has many, many billions of dollars in unclaimed assets that it's holding onto—all just waiting to be claimed. The IRS has, in the most recent tax year, about $75 million dollars worth of uncashed tax refund checks. Checks just came back, people moved, and nobody is clamoring to get their tax refunds. It is amazing to me. Other federal agencies also are holding money—FBIC, HUD, the Pension Benefit Guarantee Corp., the Treasury Department—along with individual banks, insurance companies, and other business institutions.

Now some of you might be asking: What is this unclaimed money? Where is this coming from? Well, here are some of the types of unclaimed money that are out there. Credit balances are one source. Let's say, for example, you had a credit card that you ever overpaid on. Ultimately the credit card company is supposed to send you that additional payment back.

It may take a while, but they will eventually get around to it. But what happens if you move in the meantime, or what happens if you really overpay because, say, you thought you would pay that $300 bill, and your spouse or significant other thought he would pay it, and you

Types of Missing Money and Unclaimed Funds

- Credit balances
- Dividends
- Forgotten layaway balances
- Forgotten savings and checking accounts
- Inheritances
- Insurance policies
- Military benefits
- Pension benefits
- Safe deposit box contents
- Stocks and bonds
- Tax refund checks
- Uncashed payroll checks, travelers' checks, and money orders
- Unclaimed wages and commissions
- Unused gift certificates

both wound up paying $300? The result would be a credit to your account of $300, and this is one of the ways in which unclaimed money initially gets generated.

At this point, some of you might be wondering, "How could anyone 'forget' about money that was owed to them?" Well, a couple of things could happen to cause all these sources of money to turn into unclaimed or abandoned funds.

First of all, you need to know there is a three- to five-year rule that applies to most of these funds. In essence, all the types of unclaimed property that I just mentioned are guided by time limits. If a bank or some entity has something that they know is rightfully yours and if they have not been able to connect with you and give you the refund or the insurance policy that you're due from an inheritance or whatever, after three years in most states (up to five in others) the company is required by law to turn the money over to state authorities. Then it becomes the state's responsibility.

The state takes on the role of trying to reconnect you with that money. But then a second thing occurs that causes money to go unclaimed: somebody moves, someone changes his or her name (either through marriage or divorce), or somebody dies. In the latter case, money and property can easily go unclaimed when relatives simply don't know about the existence of a deceased person's assets and accounts.

This is a huge issue in the insurance sector because insurance policies are the single biggest area of unclaimed property. I've seen statistics suggesting that as many as 20 percent of all insurance policies go unpaid. One out of five policies! That's a huge amount of unclaimed funds.

In the insurance industry there is a thing called *demutualization.* Basically, what this means is that an insurance company has gone through a reorganization. A mutual insurance company has now become a publicly owned company. What happens in those instances is that that process of demutualization generates income because stock or cash is supposed to be paid out to policyholders. Even if the deal involves only stock, even that stock holding can mean dividend payments that are due to be paid out. So if you are a policyholder with a company that has gone through a demutualization or you are a beneficiary of an insurance policy with an insurer that has gone through demutualization, you may be owed money. In the past 20 years, numerous well-known companies have gone through demutualization, at least 20 really big companies as a matter of fact. Some of them include John Hancock Financial Services, Prudential, MetLife, and Manulife, to name but a few. So if you have an insurance policy with any of these companies, I would suggest you check it out, and try to find out whether or not money is due to you.

How to Locate the Money

There are three different ways that you can go online to find out about whether or not you have some money that is due to you.

I definitely recommend that you go with the free services that will tell you whether or not there are some funds out there that you can claim.

1. The first online resource is called Missing Money (*www. missingmoney.com*). (By the way, when I checked online, I didn't come up with anything for me, but I actually did find unclaimed money for some of my family members in New York state!) It's fast and easy to use Missing Money. You type in your name and state, and you can quickly see if there are any unclaimed funds with your name on them.
2. Another good website to track down free money is at *www.unclaimed.org.*
3. Then there's an organization called the National Unclaimed Property Network. Their website is at *www.nupn.com.*

Go ahead and type in any of these three—or all three of them. Different search engines on these sites may find slightly different information, but by and large they all hook you to state and federal resources, along with insurance companies, in order for you to track down lost money. These sites make the searching process very easy for you.

There are also paid services you can use. Typically, with these, someone will send you a letter in the mail that essentially says, "I am trying to connect you with a policy or with some money that I believe is owed to you. Call me or write to this organization and let me know if you want to get the money." Once you call, they will ask for your first and last name.

A word of caution: don't ever give your Social Security number to anybody, or private information such as your driver's license or bank account data. That would be a scam, and most of these unclaimed money letters you get from reputable companies actually are not scams.

But if somebody sends you such a letter, he or she is usually what is called a *finder*. I do not have any problems with finders, especially if they are reconnecting you with money. The only drawback to using a finder is that they obviously want their cut. Some may charge as much as 30 percent of whatever the amount is that they recover. This may be a small price to pay for some of you. But others will think, as I do, that you'd much rather go with a free service where you don't have to pay anything.

When you look for unclaimed money on the free sites, don't just look under the state in which you're presenting living, especially if you've moved in recent years. Also look in places where you've previously lived, just to make sure some unclaimed funds didn't originate in those states.

If you hit the jackpot, so to speak, let me know about it. I'd love to hear from those of you who actually get unclaimed funds—and don't worry, I won't ask you for a cut!

BORROWING FOR EMERGENCIES

While these methods should only be used in dire situations, you should know you can borrow on a very short-term basis from your IRA, or on a longer-term basis from your life insurance policy.

We've talked a bit about life insurance. You can save money by raising your deductibles or you might be the beneficiary of a life insurance policy. But have you considered the value of your own life insurance policy, in particular a whole-life policy? Also known as a permanent life insurance policy, these are insurance policies that typically build up a cash value, providing an avenue you can tap for cash. You can borrow against the cash value of your permanent life insurance policy.

Also, if you have an individual retirement account, an IRA, do you know that it too can be a ready source of cash, tiding you over for 60 days if you need money? You might hear some experts in the media suggest that you cannot "borrow" from your IRA. Well, that is not exactly true. There is a provision in the law that actually says that you can take money out of your IRA as long as you replace it within 60 days. And if you do so, you will not face any tax consequences, nor will you incur the 10 percent penalties that get levied on people who take premature distributions from their IRAs (i.e., withdrawing the money before they turn 59 ½ years old).

If you ever take money out of your IRA on a short-term basis, you do have to consider the opportunity costs involved. In other words, withdrawing a given amount of money from your IRA means those funds are no longer invested and working for you. So if you had your IRA invested in, say, a stock mutual fund, and it was performing well, then withdrawing the money for 60 days means that you would miss out on any upside potential if the stock market rose during that time.

Be cautious. I generally do not recommend raiding your retirement nest egg, except under the most carefully planned, well-thought out circumstances.

All of these ideas, from leveraging your home, to finding free money on the Internet, to coming up with extra money on the job, can all put cash back into your bank account. Again, it's up to you to invest the time necessary to reap the financial rewards from these strategies. But the economic benefits are certainly worth it—especially if you use that extra cash you generate to pay down those student loans.

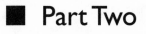 Part Two

Pay Off Student Loans

CHAPTER

MASTER SOME STUDENT LOAN BASICS

Understanding the ABCs of
Your College Loans

So you're out of college now—or perhaps just about to graduate. Congratulations! Sooner than you know it, six months will have gone by since your graduation and all of a sudden those student loan payments will come due, adding to your growing list of bills. But since you know how to budget, getting a handle on those loans will be easier than ever.

To keep yourself in good financial standing, you need to take those student loan debts seriously. I mean deadly serious, because a lapse in judgment when it comes to educational loans can prove near-fatal to your financial life. I certainly don't want to scare you, but for now just let me caution you that you don't want to mess around with the government when it comes to repaying loans for which you signed on the dotted line.

The first step on the road to financial freedom from student loans begins with having a clear understanding of where things currently stand from an economic vantage point. To that end, I'm going to help you master some student loan basics. In this chapter, you will:

- Determine what type of loans you have,
- Understand the differences between federal and private loans,
- Figure out how much you owe,
- Identify the key players in the student loan business, and
- Assess the status of your student loans

After we get through these formalities, I'll explain in subsequent chapters what you should do based on three potential scenarios:

1. You have up-to-date loans, but you'd like to lower your payments or learn how to pay them off faster;
2. Your loans are past due (i.e., delinquent), current, or in a grace period, but you absolutely cannot afford to make any payments and need to know your options; or
3. You have defaulted student loans.

Along the way, I'll also provide you with "student loan speak"— that is, I'll give you the plain English definition of certain technical words or of commonly used terminology from the student loan industry that you might find complicated, confusing, or unfamiliar.

DETERMINE WHAT TYPE OF LOANS YOU HAVE

After you earn your degree (or if you leave school for any reason, or fall below half-time enrollment status), the clock immediately starts ticking and you have anywhere from six to nine months before you must begin repayment of your student loans. Your loan provider will typically give you information about your repayment schedule and will let you know the date you are to begin repaying your college debts.

If you're starting from scratch, some of you may not recall exactly what institutions, banks, or agencies you borrowed money from, let alone how much it was or how long you're on the hook for that debt.

So your first step is to pull out your paperwork and start doing a bit of sleuthing.

You do recall all those promissory notes you signed obligating you to pay back those loans, right? Well, even if lost your paperwork amidst a move, or if you thought, "Suckers!" and gleefully chucked those promissory notes as soon as you cashed your loan checks, that doesn't absolve you of your financial responsibility. Thankfully, you can still get an accounting of what you owe and to whom.

To get a list of all your federal student loans, just hop on the Internet and use the National Student Loan Data System at *www.nslds. ed.gov*. In order to access this database, which is maintained by the Department of Education, you'll have to supply your Social Security number and date of birth to verify your identity. You'll also be required to set up a user ID and get a four-digit PIN from the Department of Education in order to access your student loan information electronically. To obtain your PIN, go to *www.pin.ed.gov*.

There's also a second online source you can utilize for information about your educational loans. It's the LoanLocator service run by the National Student Clearinghouse. To access those records, visit: *www.studentclearinghouse.org/secure_area/loan_locator.asp*. Additionally, if you're not on the Web, call the Department of Education at 1-800-621-3115 to track down your student loans.

It's important to find out what type of loans you have because your repayment options and your alternatives for handling problem loans (translation: those you've defaulted on) are determined by what types of loans you secured. The type of loan you have also determines what agency handles a defaulted loan. For instance, Federal Family Education Loans (FFEL) are handled differently than Perkins loans.

If you default on FFELs, which include Federal Stafford and Federal PLUS loans, your loans first get assigned to a guaranty agency, or an organization that administers the FFEL program for your state. The guaranty agency will then start collection activities against you. On occasion, guaranty agencies may assign loans to the Department of Education for collection. But let's say you took out federal Perkins loans. When these go into default, Perkins loans may remain with your school, or be assigned to the Department of Education for collection.

Direct loans are another story. Federal Stafford and PLUS loans are also offered through the something called the William D. Ford Direct Loan Program. You can find out more about these loans at *www. ed.gov/directloan.* When placed in default, these loans get immediately assigned to the Education Department's debt collection service.

You've no doubt heard about financial aid in the form of college grants, such as Federal Pell grants and Federal Supplemental Educational Opportunity Grants (FSEOG). Well, despite the name *grant*—which suggests that you're being given money that doesn't have to be repaid—in certain cases you might have to pay back part of a federal grant that you received while in school. Repayments are usually required if you dropped out of a program for which you were awarded a grant, or if you had an overaward, meaning the amount given to you was more than you were actually eligible to receive.

Lastly, two other types of loan you may have are Supplemental Loans for Students (SLS), and National Direct Student Loans (NDSL). If you have very old loans and none of the previously mentioned sources can find records of them, another alternative is to contact the Federal Student Aid Information Center online at *www.federalstudentaid.ed.gov* or call the center at 1-800-4-FED-AID (1-800-433-3243). They'll have your loan holder and loan history information, or can give you the address and telephone number of the agency for any loans you may have.

Knowing the type of loans you have will also help you determine how expensive (or potentially how cheap) it was to finance your college education. For instance, as of July 1, 2006, the rates on federal student loans rose to 6.8 percent from 4.77 percent. Before that time, rates were floating, meaning they could vary each year. Now that is no longer the case. Presently, the rates on Stafford Loans are fixed at that 6.8 percent level. Rates for PLUS loans—Parent Loans for University Students—are set at 8.5 percent. Because of this one change, a higher education report from the U.S. Public Interest Research Group estimates that a student who graduates with about $17,500 debt is going to pay back $5,800 more in interest with a 15-year repayment period than he or she would have previously paid, due to the higher rates.

UNDERSTAND THE DIFFERENCE BETWEEN FEDERAL AND PRIVATE LOANS

Some of you may be thinking: "But what about me? I didn't take out a federal loan. I got a private loan through a state organization, bank, or other lender." This is an increasingly common scenario.

In fact, private loans, which are funded by commercial or state sources, now total 25 percent of the dollar volume of all federal loans, $17.3 billion versus $69 billion, respectively. That's a remarkable difference from a little more than a decade ago, when the dollar value of private loans—also called alternative loans—came to just 5 percent of the volume of federal loans in the 1994–95 academic year, according to the College Board. And over the past five years, the number of private loans taken out for educational purposes has surged by an average annual rate of 27 percent. So if you took out private loans, you'll have to get information about those debts directly from the bank or institution that lent you money, or from the organization that is servicing your loans.

As a loan recipient, does it really matter if that $20,000 you borrowed came from the federal government or from a private lender? You bet your college degree it does. For starters, Perkins loans and many Stafford loans are federally subsidized, meaning the government actually helps you pay back part of the loan—by making interest payments on the loan while you're in school, during the six months after you graduate, and then further subsidizing the interest payments you later make over the life of the loan. Subsidized Stafford loans are need-based loans.

There are some federal loans, however, that are unsubsidized. These loans, including certain unsubsidized non-need-based Stafford loans, begin to accrue interest as soon as they are issued. Both subsidized and unsubsidized government loans are federally guaranteed, and both have interest rates below market levels.

By contrast, private loans are not subsidized at all. Because they're based in part on the applicant's credit history, the interest rates on private loans can vary wildly, though they currently average about 10 percent, which is higher than the rates on most federal loans. Nevertheless, the main appeal of private loans is that they've become increasingly available for students and their families who need help bridging the gap between what they can afford to pay for school and the total cost of getting that degree.

In short, private loans are more accessible for student and parents when they can't get enough grant aid or work study from school, or when they fail to secure big enough loans from the federal government.

But many experts caution students about taking on private loans unnecessarily, or without very careful consideration. Robert Shireman, executive director of the Project on Student Debt (*www.projectonstudentdebt.org*), notes that loan limits on federal loans help students from borrowing far more than they truly need. For example, dependent undergraduates are limited to a total of $23,000 in subsidized and unsubsidized federal loans while pursuing their bachelor's degrees, while independent undergraduates can borrow a total of $46,000. Meanwhile, graduate students can get a total maximum of $138,500 in subsidized and unsubsidized federal loans for their studies. But no such limits exist with private loans.

"The emergence of private student loans has created a hazardous situation where students are not getting any kind of counseling and advice about whether that loan is needed and whether that loan has good terms and conditions," says Shireman. He adds that "95 percent of those loans are variable rate loans that may or may not look good at the start but will go up if interest rates rise. They also don't have death and disability discharge options, or the hardship provisions that go with federal loans."

FIGURE OUT HOW MUCH YOU OWE

Now that you have a handle on what types of loans you have, and the differences between federal and private loans, it's time to answer a nuts-and-bolts question, namely: exactly how much do you owe? While, this may sound like a straightforward and simple question, the answer may be anything but.

Let's say you've logged on to the National Student Loan Data System (NSLDS). On the very first screen that pops up, you'll see a tab that says "Financial Aid Review." Underneath it, you'll find a line that says "Aid Summary For" followed by your name. This page summarizes the type and dollar value of each federal loan you've ever received as undergraduate, graduate, or professional student. It also lists each loan you received, in order from the most recent loan to the oldest debt. The bottom of this page says "Total All Loans" and gives you the aggregate figure for all your educational debts, including consolidated loans.

But here's where it gets tricky. You have to be sure that you don't double-count consolidated loans when you're trying to calculate how much of your loan debt you've paid off, and how much in loans you really took out while in school.

To illustrate this point, let's look at Larry Loan-Happy, who took out loans as an undergrad and graduate student in the 1990s and then consolidated his loans in 2006. Larry's information in the NSLDS might look like the one on the following page.

At first blush, you might be tempted to think that Larry borrowed $37,215 and paid off $21,468 of it, because his outstanding principal amount is $15,747. But look more closely at what really happened. Larry actually borrowed $21,000 while in school—the total of all his Stafford, Perkins, NDSL, and Supplemental loans.

After several years of repayments, he took out a loan of $16,215 to consolidate his debts. That means Larry had only paid off $4,785 of his $21,000 in loans before the consolidation. The consolidation loan paid off all of Larry's remaining debts of $16,215, and one new consolidated loan was issued for that amount.

Aid Summary for Larry Loan-Happy

Type of Loan	Loan Amount	Loan Date	Disbursed Amount	Canceled Amount	Outstanding Principal	Outstanding Interest
FFEL Consolidated	$16,215	06/05/2006	$16,215	$0	$15,747	$39
Stafford Subsidized	$7,500	10/16/1998	$7,500	$0	$0	$0
Supplemental Loan	$5,000	09/23/1998	$4,000	$0	$0	$0
National Direct Loan	$3,500	10/02/1997	$3,500	$0	$0	$0
Stafford Subsidized	$4,000	01/15/1994	$4,000	$0	$0	$0
Federal Perkins	$1,000	09/18/1993	$1,000	$0	$0	$0
Total FFEL Consol.	$16,215		$16,215	$0	$15,747	$39
Total Stafford Sub.	$11,500		$11,500	$0	$0	$0
Total Supp. Loan	$5,000		$5,000	$0	$0	$0
Total Nat. Direct	$3,500		$3,500	$0	$0	$0
Total Fed. Perkins	$1,000		$1,000	$0	$0	$0
Total All Loans	$37,215		$37,215	$0	$15,747	$39

It can be misleading to look at the bottom line numbers if you think that Larry (or, in your case, you) paid off a certain amount of debts. With a loan consolidation, another entity pays off the debt and now you owe that new lender. So in the final analysis, Larry's true borrowing amount is the "Total All Loans" line ($37,215) minus his loan consolidation figure ($16,215). That result, $21,000, is Larry's principal repayment amount.

When you see your own figures on the NSLDS, you must also net out consolidated loan figures from the total of all loans. This way you see what you have to repay, and not double-count a loan that's already been paid off on your behalf through loan consolidation. It may not surprise you very much, though, to find out that these figures are merely telling you the information as calculated for the principal balances of your loans.

To see overall true cost of your student loans over time, you'll need to use a loan repayment calculator from your lender or loan servicer. This will tell you how much extra in interest you'll pay on your loans by financing this debt over time. In most cases, student loan balances double or even triple when extended over typical 10-, 20-, or 30-year repayment periods.

One final thing you should know about the information maintained online is that the National Student Loan Data System is a repository of information from multiple sources. So any changes to the data are made by those sources. Always check your promissory notes and original loan documentation against what's contained in the NSLDS database. If you notice that your paperwork is different—let's say it contains a smaller loan amount or a different loan disbursement date—from what is in the NSLDS records, take immediate action to reconcile that discrepancy. To get info in the NSLDS fixed or updated, contact your school, lender, servicer, or guaranty agency as appropriate—but not the NSLDS.

IDENTIFY THE KEY PLAYERS IN THE STUDENT LOAN BUSINESS

It's easy to get confused by the hodgepodge of players in the world of student loans. For the purposes of managing and paying off your loans, though, you mainly need to understand the role of three distinct players: your loan servicer, your lender, and the guaranty agency on your loans.

In the course of writing this book, I looked up the information contained in the National Student Loan Data System on my old college debts. For my loans, Sallie Mae was listed as the servicer, JP Morgan as the lender, and the California Student Aid Commission as the guaranty agency on the loans. But what exactly does this mean?

Well, the current servicer is the organization that manages a loan for a lender or a school. The servicer's job is to compute interest on your student loans and mail regular billing statements to you. This is why you're probably far more familiar with your loan servicer than you are with your actual lender. In fact, you may have even forgotten (or perhaps never really knew) who the lender on your loan was. That's a far cry from other debts you might have. Think for a moment about that Visa card in your wallet. You probably know off the top of your head which bank issued it—whether it was MBNA, Capital One, Citibank, or some other financial entity.

The lender for your student loans, as you might suspect, is the institution that actually holds the promissory note you signed when you agreed to take out the loan. It's the lender you are legally obligated to repay—not your loan servicer. So even though you might cut checks to a loan servicer like Sallie Mae month after month, that money is officially owed to your lender. (In Sallie Mae's case, Sallie Mae is actually a lender, too; in fact, it's the largest holder of student loans in the nation.)

Finally, the guaranty agency on your loan, as the name suggests, is the agency that guarantees repayment of your loan to the lender. If you don't pay up, it's the guaranty agency's responsibility to step in and pay off most, if not all, of your loan, satisfying the lender's financial claims.

ASSESS THE STATUS OF YOUR LOANS

According to the NSLDS, information about Pell grants is updated daily; new loan information is recorded within 30 days and loans that you're currently repaying may be as much as 120 days old. Your loan servicer usually can to give you the most up-to-date information about loan balances, payoff amounts, and so on.

When you're online at the NSLDS database, you can find the following information:

- The type of loan(s) you received
- The loan amount and loan date
- The cancelled amount (if any)
- The outstanding principal
- The outstanding interest
- The total amount of each category of loan you received (such as direct loans, Stafford loans, or Perkins loans)

You'll probably have more than one loan. So if you do have multiple college debts, you can click on each loan and get even more detailed information, such as the date you entered repayment, the school you were attending while you obtained the loan, and—most importantly—the status of your loans.

More specifically, you'll find a two-letter code that describes the loan status for each educational loan you received. RP for instance, is the abbreviated code for a loan "in repayment." At first glance, you might be inclined to think that there are just a handful of codes describing the statuses associated with a student loan: like a loan that's being repaid or has already been paid in full, a loan that's delinquent or in default, a loan that's been deferred or a loan in forbearance, or a consolidated loan. In reality, there are nearly four dozen categories to describe the status of various student loans. Here they are:

After you see how your loans are classified, you should pick up the phone immediately and call the Department of Education, your

Loan Status	Status Description
AL	Abandoned loan
BC	Bankruptcy claim—discharged
BK	Bankruptcy claim—active
CA	Canceled
DA	Deferred
DB	Defaulted then bankrupt, Chapter 13—active
DC	Defaulted—compromise

DD	Defaulted then died
DE	Death
DF	Defaulted—unresolved
DI	Disability
DK	Defaulted then bankrupt, Chapter 13—discharged
DL	Defaulted—in litigation
DN	Defaulted then paid in full through a consolidated loan
DO	Defaulted then bankrupt—active, other
DP	Defaulted—paid in full
DR	Defaulted loan included in rolled-up loan
DS	Defaulted then disabled
DT	Defaulted—collection terminated
DU	Defaulted—unresolved
DW	Defaulted—write-off
DX	Defaulted—six consecutive payments
DZ	Defaulted—six consecutive payments, then missed payment(s)
FB	Forbearance
FC	False certification discharge
IA	Loan originated
ID	In school or grace period
IG	In grace period
IM	In military grace
IP	In postdeferment grace period
OD	Defaulted then bankrupt—discharged, other
PC	Paid in full through consolidation loan
PF	Paid in full
PM	Presumed paid in full
PN	Nondefaulted, paid in full through consolidated loan
RF	Refinanced
RH	Loan transferred by Debt Collection System to Sallie Mae
RP	In repayment
UA	Temporarily uninsured—no default claim requested
UB	Temporarily uninsured—default claim denied
UC	Permanently uninsured/unreinsured—no default claim requested
UD	Permanently uninsured/unreinsured—default claim denied
UI	Unreinsured
XD	Defaulted—six consecutive payments

Source: National Student Loan Data System (NSLDS) for Students

lender, or servicer if any of the following situations are applicable:

- You find what you believe is erroneous or incomplete information about your loan.
- You discover loans that you never took out or didn't authorize.
- You have any loan currently in default.
- You have questions about why a given loan is classified a certain way.

In 2005–06, undergraduate students borrowed nearly $19.9 billion through the federal subsidized Stafford loan program, plus an additional $16.6 billion via the unsubsidized Stafford loan program. Out of the $69 billion in federal loans, students borrowed 86 percent of those funds, with PLUS loans account for the remaining 14 percent of loans made. PLUS loans are awarded to the parents of university students and, beginning in 2006–07, PLUS loans also became available to graduate students.

No matter what kind of loan you (or your parents) obtain, you always want to keep it in good standing. In the next chapter, learn how to pay down your student loan debt.

5

PAY NOW

Smart Options to Drastically Reduce Those Student Loan Bills

Repaying student loans, while a financial hardship for many, can be done at some level by practically all borrowers if you have some income. The options presented in this chapter assume that:

1. You have a job, and
2. You can afford at least $5 a month to spend on your student loans.

If neither of those criteria describes your circumstances, you've got bigger problems than just student loans. And the prescription for what ails you—at least as it pertains to your college debt dilemma—will likely be found in later chapters. For now, though, I'm going to assume that you have some level of income, no matter how modest, and that you can pay back something on your student loans, but you just want it to be a comfortable amount each month, not something that stresses you out every paycheck.

Happily, there are several options to reducing your student loan bills—both in the short term and in the long run. The key question is:

What kind of relief do you most need? Are you desperately short of cash right now and in dire need of drastically lowering your current student loan bills? Then you'll likely pick a payment plan that will allow you to stretch your student loans out over a longer time period. That will give you instant financial relief, but it will also increase the total amount of your repayments in the long run, because you'll be paying finance charges over an extended time frame.

Remember when you were in school, and you had some college professor who put practically everything in terms of a formula? Well, if you had to express your student loan repayment options as a formula, it would look something like this:

Lower payments today = extra monthly cash now + additional
future finance charges
Higher payments today = less available cash now + fewer
finance charges in the future

There's always a trade-off, depending on what objective you'd like to accomplish. Easier payments in the short run (i.e., today) mean more money in the long run. This holds true no matter what type of student debt you have—federal loans or private loans. As long as you understand that basic premise, which is at the root of all student loan repayment scenarios, you can make the best choice as to how to proceed based on your individual circumstances.

If you have private loans, I'll describe your repayment options at the end of this chapter. For now, let's address those federal loans, which are the most common form of college debt. To begin with, there are four different types of repayment plans for your federal student loans:

1. Standard repayment
2. Extended repayment
3. Graduated repayment
4. Income contingent repayment

If you're a student, you can choose any of the four plans. But for parents with PLUS loans, only the first three plans are available. The same thing applies to direct loans: you can only select the standard, extended, or graduated repayment options. Also, don't worry about being locked into one plan for life. You are permitted to switch from one plan to another, depending on your financial status.

Now let's look closely at how each of these differs, and at which plans are best for college graduates in various situations.

STANDARD LOAN REPAYMENT PLANS

Under a standard repayment plan, your monthly payment amount is fixed for a loan term as long as ten years. That might sound like a long time. But it's actually the shortest time frame available out of all the repayment options. You have the option, however, of prepaying any of your student loans if you're particularly flush with cash. However, most college grads will need ten years, and then some, to fully repay their college debts. Depending on how much money you borrowed in school, it's possible that your loan term could be shorter than ten years. But no matter how many years it takes you to repay your obligations, with the standard repayment plan you must make payments of at least $50 a month until your loans are paid in full.

If you come out of school, land a high-paying job, and have managed to keep your other expenses fairly low, the standard repayment plan is your best bet. This is the plan that will let you pay off your student loans fastest and with the least amount of money paid in interest.

Standard payment plans also offer the best interest rate out of all the plans available.

To give you a sense of what the average college grad might pay, coming out of school with $20,000 in debt, I've used one of the online college loan calculators found on FinAid's Web site (*www.finaid.org/calculators*). All of the analyses in this chapter have been calculated on FinAid's Web site to demonstrate the difference in these types of loans. However, there are many other calculators out there, and your lender can also assist you with the math.

Here's what the FinAid calculator showed:

Standard Loan Calculator

Loan Balance	$20,000
Loan Interest Rate	6.80%
Loan Term	10 years
Minimum Payment	$50.00
Monthly Loan Payment	$230.16
Number of Payments	120
Cumulative Payments	$27,619.31
Total Interest Paid	$7,619.31

In this projection, the monthly loan payment was calculated at 119 payments of $230.16 plus a final payment of $230.27. According to FinAid, it's estimated that you'd need to earn at least $27,619.20 a year in order to afford to repay this loan. That estimate assumes you'll be spending 10 percent of your gross monthly income on student loans. But if you earned far less than that $27,619.20 figure, remember that your payments can be as little as $50 a month with the standard repayment option. (Thus the FinAid "Minimum Payment" amount show is $50). Also, the results above assume you're paying interest charges on any unsubsidized loans while you're in school. If you're not and if the interest is capitalizing, or being added to your outstanding balance, your total payments would be higher than the estimates above.

EXTENDED REPAYMENT OPTION

An extended repayment plan is intended to give college grads a little breathing room in repaying their student loans. This payment option lets you pay off your college debt in as little as 12 years or as many as 30 years, depending on how much money you borrowed while in school.

As previously stated, any time you lengthen your payment term, you're automatically tacking on additional finance charges for the privilege of carrying that debt for extra years and making smaller monthly payments. Under the extended payment plan, your minimum monthly payments will be $50, just like with the standard option, but you have longer to knock out your debts. By stretching out your payment term, the extended option gives you a short-term financial break so you don't blow your whole budget on student loan payments.

The extended plan is best used when your income is low or when you've had a series of financial problems that truly call for you to stretch out your student loan debt. Because you'll be tacking on extra finance charges in the long run, you have to weigh the long-term cost of doing that against the short-term benefit to your bank account in the here and now.

The worst thing you can do with an extended plan, however, is put your student loan debt on autopilot and just forget about it. I made this mistake for years to be honest. I had a very comfortable $186 a month student loan payment that I stretched out unnecessarily even when I could afford to make larger payments. I did pay extra—from time to time whenever I thought about it. But for the most part I simply let the payments remain on automatic deduction from my bank account and I didn't give them a second thought. A smarter strategy is to stay on top of your student loans and, even if you have the luxury of paying a smaller amount because you're on an extended payment plan, go ahead and make additional payments when feasible. This will save you lots of time and money in the long run.

Some of you may be thinking: "Thirty years! I don't want my student loans to turn into a mortgage." That's smart thinking. For many college grads, especially those of you with six-figure debts outstanding, an extended payment plan may be the most affordable option available. The upside is: by elongating those payments over so many years, you quite naturally are going to decrease the monthly amount that you're shelling out in the present time. If you've got large credit card debts, kids, medical bills, and many other financial obligations, an extended repayment plan is something to consider seriously.

Are you ready for the black-and-white numbers about how much more you'll pay by extending the life of your student loans? Look at the following analysis:

Extended Loan Calculator

Loan Balance	$20,000
Loan Interest Rate	6.80%
Loan Term	20 years
Minimum Payment	$50.00
Monthly Loan Payment	$152.67
Number of Payments	240
Cumulative Payments	$36,639.74
Total Interest Paid	$16,639.74

Source: FinAid

In this scenario, the monthly loan payment was calculated at 239 payments of $152.67 plus a final payment of $151.61. To swing these payments, you'll need to earn a minimum annual salary of $18,320.40, assuming you want to devote 10 percent of your pay to repaying your student loans. Note how using a loan term of 20 years, instead of the standard 10-year repayment plan, reduces your monthly loan payment by $77.49, or 33.7 percent. The bad news is that it also increases your total interest paid by $9,020.46, or 118.4 percent.

GRADUATED REPAYMENT PROGRAM

In contrast to the standard and extended repayment plans, the graduated repayment plan lets you ease into your student loan payments. This program begins with very low payments, which gradually increase every two years. When you start out on this plan, your payments will be equal to either just the interest on your loan, or half of the payment you'd make on a standard payment plan.

The loan term for a graduated repayment plan lasts anywhere from 12 to 30 years, based on your total borrowing. And there are a few rules you should be aware of concerning graduated repayments. Your monthly payment can never be less than 50 percent of the minimum amount payable under a standard repayment. And because the standard plan carries a $50 a month minimum repayment, this means you must always pay at least $25 a month with a graduated repayment option. On top of that, your payment with a graduated repayment plan can't total more than 150 percent of the monthly payment under the standard repayment plan.

The graduated payment plan often works best if you graduated from college but are only making a modest wage and expect your income to keep rising slowly but surely. So let's say your payment started off at $150 a month. After two years, it could go up 10 percent to $165 a month. And then two years later, it could go up again to around $180. Your payments would keep rising, helping you pay off debts faster than the extended repayment option, but slower than the ten-year standard plan.

Take a look at the repayment table on the next page for extended and graduated loan repayment plans. It shows the maximum number of years you can take to pay off your student loans, based on the amount of funds you borrowed.

Graduated/Extended Repayment Table

Amount of Debt	Maximum Repayment Period
Less than $10,000	12 years
$10,000–$19,999	15 years
$20,000–$39,999	20 years
$40,000–$59,999	25 years
$60,000 or more	30 years

Again, even if you take a 20- or 25-year repayment plan, you can pay off any federal student loan early without any penalties. As long as your loan isn't in default, here's how any "extra" payments get applied. The additional payment first gets applied to interest and then toward the principal. I've heard with great dismay of many former students who've made additional payments on their student loans only to be totally discouraged months or years later when they don't see their balances declining. In many cases what's happening is that those extra payments are being improperly applied—or at least they're not being applied in the way the college grads intended.

Take a look now at the results of paying off a $20,000 student loan balance in 20 years using the graduated repayment method.

These results assume that you're paying the interest charges on any unsubsidized loans and not capitalizing the interest while in school. If this wasn't the case, your cumulative payments and interest charges would be higher than shown here in this approximation.

Graduated Repayment Calculator

Loan Balance	$20,000
Loan Interest Rate	8.25%
Loan Term	20 years
Months Per Adjustment Period	24
Initial Loan Payment	$137.50
Final Loan Payment	$241.30
Cumulative Payments	$38,632.15
Total Interest Paid	$18,632.15

Source: FinAid

Notice how the graduated repayment plan would result in you paying a total of $38,632.15, including $18,632.15 worth of interest. That compares slightly more favorably to the extended repayment option, which also lasts for 20 years, but has you shelling out a cumulative total of $40,899.15, including total interest charges of $20,899.15.

Paying Extra to Get Ahead

If you make more money at any point in your career than you expected, please go ahead and make bigger student loan payments. If the money's really flowing, you'll barely miss an extra $100 or $200 every month. But applying those funds wisely can really help to knock down your student loan balances more quickly.

When you send in an additional payment that is one month's worth of your student loan bill or greater, you have to include a note specifically saying that you want the extra funds applied to your principal, to reduce your principal balance outstanding. If you don't, your extra payment gets treated as merely a payment in advance of the due date, and your lender will put off your next payment due date as appropriate. Obviously, this does nothing to knock down your principal faster, thereby slashing your interest charges over time. Don't let this little quirk of the system wreck your best financial efforts. Be smart about your extra payments, and send that letter as required.

Both of these plans, of course, are trumped financially by the standard repayment plan, which—with a 10-year repayment schedule-has monthly payments of $245.31, cumulative payments of $29,436.63, and total interest of $9,436.63.

INCOME CONTINGENT REPAYMENT PLANS

When you pay off your student loans based on the income contingent repayment plan, your monthly payments are based strictly on your income and the amount of debt you had. Your monthly payments also fluctuate annually as your income changes. Income contingent plans let you take as long as 25 years. And these loans feature a unique characteristic not found in any of the other loan programs: after 25 years worth of payments, whatever you owe is written off—you don't have to pay it!

That may sound like a great deal. And perhaps it could be—if the law concerning student loans gets changed in the future. For now, however, under current regulations, any amount of your student loan debt that gets written off by the government after your 25-year repayment is considered taxable income to you. So you could be 55 or 60 years old, expecting to finally be rid of your college debt burden, when the government has one last nasty financial surprise in store for you. Imagine what a shock that must be to some people who actually pay their loans for decades and then get hit with taxes on the written-off portion of their student loans!

With an income contingent plan, you must make payments of at least $5 a month. Because of how interest is treated within income contingent repayment plans, experts say you should not prepay these loans, unlike the other three types of student loan repayment programs. If you'd like to move from one plan to another, you're allowed to swap out of repayment plan once a year, provided the maximum loan term for the new plan is longer than the amount of time your loans have already been in repayment. For example, let's say you signed up long ago for a 30-year extended payment plan, and now you're in year 27 of the plan. You can't switch into the 25-year income contingent repayment plan and have the remaining balance written off. The government won't fall for that.

Income contingent payment plans are appropriate if you have seasonal work, income that varies wildly from time to time, or if you work on commissions that can be difficult to predict. By using an income-sensitive plan, you'll be protected from any downturns in your financial life if you or your business isn't earning as much money as you'd hoped.

Because this method of repayment is based on your income—no matter how small it might be—the positive part of this program is that you should always be able to afford your student loan bills. The downside to this repayment plan, though, is that if you have a really good year or some really high-earning months, your student loans will likely take a chunk out of money you'd probably like to use or enjoy in some other fashion.

Other individuals who might want to consider an income contingent repayment plan are those who have specific prospects for higher incomes in the future. This might be if you know you're getting married, for example, and in a year from now your income combined with your spouse's will be higher than it is now. Or maybe you're in an apprentice-type program on your job, and if you successfully complete your training you'll get a pay raise next year. In these types of scenarios, you might find comfort in using the income contingent repayment method to pay down your student loan debt.

You may recall that I said earlier in this chapter that all four loan repayment options were available to students, but that for parents with PLUS loans the income contingent plan was not available. Can you guess why that is? I dare say it's because the income contingent plan is the only one with the government write-off provision. And you can bet your bottom dollar that the government's bean counters have done all kinds of actuarial studies and analyses to look at mortality rates and things of that nature to see when a borrower is apt to die, retire, get on Social Security, and things of that nature.

Who do you think is likely to live longer: you or your parents? If you're a student and you guessed yourself, you get a pat on the back. Now who is likely to go into retirement first? If you said your parents, right again. I don't think the government wants parents, who might be in their 40s, 50s, or 60s when their children are in college, having to pay back loans for 25 years throughout their retirement. On the other hand, they probably wouldn't want the risk of that older American dying before he or she has a chance to pay off that loan.

Here's a calculation of what your monthly payments would look like, assuming you had $20,000 in college loans, used an income contingent repayment plan, and started out making an annual salary of $50,000, which rose to $65,000 five years later.

Interestingly, if you had a much lower salary, say $30,000 instead

Income Contingent Repayment Calculator - $50,000 Starting Salary

Total Graduating Debt	$20,000.00	
Initial AGI	$50,000.00	
Income Growth Rate	4.00%	
Weighted Average Interest Rate	8.25%	
Discount Rate	5.80%	
ICR Interest Rate Discount	2.00%	after 48 months
Interest Rate Discount	0.80%	after 12 months

	Income Contingent	Fixed Monthly Repayment
Years in Repayment	11.2 years	21.3 years
Minimum Payment	$5.00	$50.00
First Payment	$219.24	$157.69
Total Amount Paid	$29,605.84	$40,182.33
Total Interest Paid	$9,605.84	$20,182.33
Total Accrued Interest	$9,605.84	$20,182.33
Total Government Write-off	$0.00	$0.00
NPV of Total Paid	$21,913.71	$23,331.85
NPV of Gov. Write-off	$0.00	$0.00

Source: FinAid

of $50,000 annually, and you predicted that your income would rise to $39,000 after five years, your monthly repayment plan wouldn't look all that different. The monthly payment would drop by just $43.87. But with a lower salary, the total amount of interest you paid would rise by $3,303.77. This is because with income-sensitive plans, higher wage earners actually pay a larger percentage of their income toward student loan debt, and lower-wage earners pay a smaller percentage of income toward college loans—ultimately resulting in lower-paid workers doling out more in finance charges in the long run, as the following table shows.

Before you choose any plan, do take the time to run some numbers on a college loan calculator. You can use the FinAid calculator or get other experts, such as financial aid officers or college loan counselors, to run some numbers for you and give you the results of various payment

Income Contingent Repayment Plan—$30,000 Starting Salary

Total Graduating Debt	$20,000.00	
Initial AGI	$30,000.00	
Income Growth Rate	4.00%	
Weighted Average Interest Rate	8.25%	
Discount Rate	5.80%	
ICR Interest Rate Discount	2.00%	after 48 months
Interest Rate Discount	0.80%	after 12 months

	Income Contingent	Fixed Monthly Repayment
Years in Repayment	14.7 years	21.3 years
Minimum Payment	$5.00	$50.00
First Payment	$175.37	$157.69
Total Amount Paid	$32,909.61	$40,182.33
Total Interest Paid	$12,909.61	$20,182.33
Total Accrued Interest	$12,909.61	$20,182.33
Total Government Write-off	$0.00	$0.00
NPV of Total Paid	$22,181.14	$23,331.85
NPV of Gov. Write-off	$0.00	$0.00

Source: FinAid

plan options. Whatever student loan repayment plan you settle on, make sure you select a lender that rewards you for being a good customer.

Paying on time not only saves you money (in finance charges in the long run), it can also lower your monthly rate in the short-term because many companies give you a break on the interest rate for timely payments. So set up an automatic deduction to get those payments in consistently, and on time. Having an automatic debit of your checking or savings account will also entitle you to get a break from your lender. If not, call them up and ask why not—let them know you will take your loans elsewhere if they don't shave your interest rate at least ¼ percent. In fact, many lenders will cut your student loan interest rate by 2 percent after 48 consecutive on-time payments. On Federal Direct Consolidated Loans, you get an 0.8 percent interest rate decrease after 12 months. Loan company My Rich Uncle (*www.myrichuncle.com*) in 2006 became the first lender to ever cut up to 1.25% off the governments fixed rate on federal Stafford loans and 2% federal PLUS loan upfront at the time of repayment.

PLAY "LET'S MAKE A DEAL"

Consolidation can factor into your different repayment options. I'll touch on it briefly here, but turn to Chapter 6 for a more in-depth look at the pros and cons. In order to consolidate your federal student loans, you must be in your six-month grace period or already repaying your loans. You have the right to consolidate a wide variety of college debts including:

- Stafford loans (subsidized or unsubsidized)
- Perkins loans
- PLUS loans
- Health Professions Student Loans (HPSL)
- Health Education Assistance Loans (HEAL)
- Nursing Student Loans (NSL)
- National Direct Student Loans (NDSL)
- SLS Loans (formerly ALAS Loans)

Loan consolidation should never be done on the fly, without some serious comparison shopping to make sure that you're getting the best terms and benefits from a lender. Ask what rebates, discounts, interest-rate reductions, and other perks a lender might offer you as a borrower prior to signing up with any institution. Before you consolidate with any lender, it's vitally important to make sure that consolidation is your best course of action. Consolidating loans can lower your monthly payments, but, as previously mentioned, it can also cause you to lose some benefits, such as deferment or forbearance privileges with Perkins loans.

Also remember that when you consolidate loans, the new interest

> **A**sk for These Perks from Your Lender
>
> _____
>
> • Interest rate reduction for automatic deductions
> • Lowered interest rate for on-time payments
> • Reduced or eliminated loan origination fees
> • Cash rebates or reduced fees for good payers

rate you get won't necessarily be the lowest rate you currently have. Rather, any new consolidated loan you get will be a fixed, weighted average based on all the loans you consolidated. The interest rate will be rounded up to the next $1/8$ percent from that weighted average, and capped at 8.25 percent by federal regulations. While you can't consolidate private loans through the federal loan consolidation, you can consolidate federal loans that are in any repayment plan—whether they're currently paid via the standard, extended, graduated or income contingent method. And when you consolidate any of these loans, your repayment plan will be anywhere from 10 to 30 years, depending on the amount of your debt.

If you're having difficulty with your payments, and you're in the process of consolidating loans, you can ask for your lender to temporarily stop your payments while your consolidation loan is being processed, giving you a little wiggle room financially.

NEGOTIATE YOUR OWN MONTHLY PAYMENT

Besides consolidating your loans, there is another underused method to lower your monthly student loan payments when you're cash-strapped. It's not very talked about, and most college grads have no idea this option is available to them. I'm talking about negotiating with the federal government for a reduced monthly payment. Many people mistakenly think this is not possible. But the truth of the matter is that it is not only possible, it's perfectly acceptable under federal law. You just have to learn how the system works, which is exactly what I'm about to reveal.

Let's say your finances are really tight because you got sick and had medical bills that your insurance company wouldn't cover. Moreover, you have two children. They're both under five years old and one of them has special needs. So you pay for day care expenses every week and for a highly skilled, reliable, and experienced caregiver/ special education teacher to watch the kids while you work.

And let's also add into the mix that you live in a rural area—or maybe even in a big city—but you have one whopper of a commute to work, so your transportation costs are much higher than normal. (By the way: commutes of an hour or more are increasingly common. I used to have a crazy commute—2 ½ hours each way from Philadelphia to New York via Amtrak each day. Mercifully, that was before my kids were born.)

In any event, my point is that you don't have a cookie-cutter life that fits nicely into some government prescribed formula about what your "normal" monthly expense are or should be. If your lifestyle happens to be expensive—and I'm not talking about because you're buying designer bags or living high on the hog—then you may be able to get some relief from the Department of Education.

The secret lies in obtaining and properly filling out one critical form called a Statement of Financial Status. This form isn't particularly onerous; it's just two pages, plus one page of instructions. You can find it online at the Department of Education: *www.ed.gov/offices/ OSFAP/DCS/forms/fs.pic.pdf.*

To complete the form, you'll be asked to declare your income and show evidence of it with two paycheck stubs and two years worth of tax returns. You'll also need to list all your monthly bills, itemizing what you owe to whom and in what amounts. If you make quarterly or annual payments—on things like auto insurance or property taxes—break that down into a monthly amount and include that in your tally of monthly expenditures.

The Statement of Financial Status asks for pertinent identifying information, such as your Social Security number. The Department of Education also requests the name, phone number, and address of your employer. To some of you, this may seem like a big hassle. But it's nothing like the much greater hassle you could face down the road (keep reading about wage garnishments) if you get behind on your student loan payments and find yourself on the wrong side of the Department of Education. A much better alternative is to simply ask for help now.

State your case to the Department of Education as clearly and concisely as you can, letting the numbers speak for themselves. If your debts are unusually high, it can't hurt to include a brief statement—no more than one page, perhaps two at most—explaining the particulars of your circumstances. And here's a key point: make sure you know what the average costs are for various expenses in your region, like food, housing, transportation, and so on. You can find out this information by going to the website of the IRS. Check out the link at: *www.irs.gov/individuals/article/0,,id=96543,00.html.*

If your expenses are out of whack with regional or national averages, be sure to state why it is that your costs are much higher. Don't just leave it up to some loan officer to look at the numbers alone and make a determination about you as if you were just a statistic. Give them a glimpse into the real life issues you're facing and your dire financial straits—without going overboard or being unnecessarily dramatic about things.

One of the best parts about this Statement of Financial Status is that the Department of Education puts you in the driver's seat. They ask you what's reasonable for you given your circumstances. They ask you to say how much you can afford to pay—and to show good faith by sending in a check for that amount. So the next step is for you to do just that: submit your statement and accompanying check for the proposed amount of the monthly payment you'd like, adhering to their rules precisely in all regards. Don't send cash; use a check or money order and write your Social Security number on it. I recommend that you mail the statement and check through the U.S. Postal Service, sending it certified mail, return receipt requested, to this address:

U.S. Department of Education
PO Box 4169
Greenville, TX 75403-4169

After this, it's a waiting game. You'll just have to sit tight and wait to get the department's response. If you've done a good job of documenting your expenses, and explaining why your bills are higher than normal, you should receive exactly what you requested. At the very least, you'll get a smaller payment than what your lender, guaranty agency, or the Department of Education originally sought.

LET UNCLE SAM HELP

One thing you can count on is getting a little help from the government in other ways as it pertains to student loans. For parents in particular, you and your child may be entitled to deduct from your taxes up to $2,500 of the annual interest you pay on student loans.

Under current IRS guidelines, even if you don't itemize, you can take the full write-off if your annual income is $105,000 or less and you and your spouse file jointly. You can claim a partial deduction if your income falls below $135,000. For single tax filers, the income limits are $50,000 and $65,000, respectively in order to qualify for the full or partial deductions. This tax break can save you big bucks: as much as $1,875 over five years for those of you in the 15 percent bracket; and up to $3,500 if you're in the 28 percent bracket.

And here's another tax break for parents. If you tapped the equity in your home to help fund your child's college education—an increasingly common way parents are paying higher education costs—then you can claim a tax deduction for that as well. Homeowners are allowed to deduct up to $100,000 for interest paid on mortgage loans. You can claim this write-off as long as you itemize your deductions. And hey, there's nothing wrong with letting Uncle Sam underwrite the cost of your (or your child's) college education. We all pay our fair share of taxes and make all kinds of other contributions to society. Why shouldn't college grads and their parents take advantage of every available financial break they have coming?

PAY OFF PRIVATE LOANS

While there are four universal repayment options for federal student loans, repayment options vary from lender to lender in the world of private loans. Generally speaking though, you have fewer repayment alternatives with private loans.

Repay Principal and Interest Immediately

All private lenders offer you the chance to repay your student loans immediately. In most cases, your begin paying the debt 30 to 45 days after your loan is disbursed. This is the fastest way to eliminate your college loans and the best option to lower your overall student loan debt because you'll greatly reduce your interest charges by paying your debts immediately and not deferring any part of your payments.

Unfortunately, this option is the most rarely used one for students. Financial aid counselors say that 90 percent of all students elect to defer payments while they're enrolled in school, according to a report called "The Future of Private Loans: Who Is Borrowing and Why" from the Institute for Higher Education Policy.

Defer Principal and Make Interest-Only Payments

Other private lenders permit you to make interest-only payments while you are a student, and defer making payments on the principal balance of your loans. If you can afford it, this is the next best option if you want to limit your overall student loan debt. By making interest-only payments while enrolled in school you eliminate the process by which unpaid interest is *capitalized*, or added to your total loan balance. The interest on some loans is capitalized quarterly and at the beginning of repayment. This is the case, for instance, with private loans provided by the Student Loan Network Program, which is backed by PNC Bank. With other private lenders, the interest on your loans will be capitalized one time, when you begin making payments. This is the case with private educational loans offered through Citibank.

Defer Principal and Interest and Pay Nothing While in School

A third option commonly offered by private lenders lets you make no payments whatsoever while you are a student, deferring both the principal and interest on your loans. Again, this is the most commonly chosen path taken by students and it's easy to see why. This is often presented as the no-hassle option, which undoubtedly appeals to cash-strapped, busy students who may or may not be working. Among those students who are employed, their earnings are likely being used to pay living expenses or other necessities. So this "pay nothing now" option holds tremendous appeal.

It's also the repayment option heavily marketed by private lenders who emphasize the ease and convenience of their student loans. But before you choose this option, make sure you run the numbers so that you see what you total loan amount will be upon graduation—after you've deferred all payments for four years or more.

So assume you borrowed $10,000 in private loans, paid $471.20 in loan fees, and deferred all payments while you were a student. With capitalized interest added to your student loans, your $10,000 loan balance skyrockets to $14,864.94. This is your new principal loan amount, sometimes called principal at repayment. This figure represents the original loan amount you originally requested, plus loan

> ## The High Cost of Deferred Payments and Capitalized Interest
>
> Many people with student loans defer making interest and principal payments until after graduation, and then are stunned to see how much their college debt has grown. The reason for this sticker shock: capitalized interest gets added to your original student loan balance. This is particularly common if you have private student loans, because they aren't subsidized, meaning the government isn't paying the interest on your loans while you're in school, as is the case with federal loans.

fees, plus interest that has been capitalized and added to the loan. If you take 20 years to pay off this loan, you'll pay an additional $21,764 in interest, for a total repayment amount of $31,764, according to figures from CollegeLoanSolutions.com.

By repaying immediately and not deferring your payments, you can slash your interest charges by 45 percent—to just $12,022.40.

OTHER PROS AND CONS
OF PRIVATE LOANS

Loan cancellations and loan forgiveness options are nonexistent with private lenders. Additionally, while many private lenders offer deferments (and sometimes forbearance at their own discretion), deferments aren't legally mandated, as is the case with federal loans if you meet certain requirements. Still, the ease with which private loans can be obtained is attractive to many students and families. In most cases, you just pick up the phone to call a lender, or fill out a simple application online, and you'll know within minutes whether you're approved for a private loan. Some private loans have maximum dollar limits while others let you borrow up to the total cost of your education. It's worthwhile, therefore, to be judicious in obtaining these loans. Only borrow what you truly need.

Another point to consider: loan origination fees on private educational loans can be very steep. A loan origination fee is a charge a lender imposes for *originating* or processing a loan. Currently, loan origination fees range from 0 percent to 3 percent on federal loans. But loan origination fees on private loans can range from nothing to 10.5 percent or more, depending on the loan type, your credit, the repayment option you select, and whether or not you have a co-signer. For example, as of early 2007, the JPMorgan Chase Education One loan for undergraduates carries a 3.0 percent to 10.5 percent loan origination fee, which is added to and financed with your loan.

Even if you took out more costly private loans, with higher interest rates or more expensive fees, rest assured that you can still pay off your college debts. By utilizing all the strategies detailed in *Zero Debt for College Grads*, you'll be in great shape to eliminate those student loans in the quickest manner possible, yet at a pace that is doable for you given all your other financial obligations. Clearly, the costs of obtaining federal and private loans and then paying them off over a number of years can quickly add up. If you have multiple loans outstanding, it can also be a taxing job to keep track of all your paperwork and maintain up-to-date information your college debts. Some people make this process more manageable by consolidating their student loans. In the next chapter, you'll learn about the benefits and drawbacks of consolidating your college loans. Armed with that information, you'll be able to decide if consolidation is right for you.

6

THE PROS AND CONS OF LOAN CONSOLIDATION

*Should You Roll All Your Loans
into One?*

Some college grads with enormous college debt see loan consolidation as a panacea. While it's true that loan consolidation can significantly lower your monthly payments, you also need to be smart about deciding whether consolidation is really right for you. In this chapter, we'll take a look at the relative benefits and drawbacks of loan consolidation so that you can make an informed choice about whether this option is desirable or even necessary.

As explained in the previous chapter, loan consolidation is the process by which an entity such as a bank pays off your existing student loan debts, and rolls all those loans into one bigger loan. In most cases, you have the option of stretching your payments out over many years, indeed across many decades, and the result is that the monthly amount you have to shell out is greatly reduced. Beyond those basics, however, there are lots of intricacies governing loan consolidation. There are so many details to know about consolidation, in fact, that this whole chapter is devoted to explaining the myriad options, benefits, and pitfalls of consolidating your student loans. It's my hope that this chapter will answer some of the most pressing questions you may have about loan consolidation.

ELIGIBILITY RULES AND OTHER REQUIREMENTS

One extremely important fact you should know at the outset is that as of July 1, 2006, a rash of changes went into effect that, in various ways, affected all federal student loans. And sure enough, consolidated federal student loans were among those impacted by the new rules. For instance, before that date, married couples could combine their student loans into one big loan and repay that debt jointly. Now married couples can no longer obtain a direct consolidation loan as joint borrowers. (This is for the best, in my opinion. Consider what happens if you should divorce from your spouse. If you had a consolidated loan, you and your ex would be individually and jointly on the hook for each other's debts—regardless of who racked up those student loans!)

Another big change in the law, as of July 1, 2006, is that federal student loans switched from variable rate loans to loans with fixed interest rates. Just a year or two ago you may have been able to consolidate a federal student loan and lock in an extremely low interest rate of 3 or 4 percent. This is no longer the case. With the new law, any Stafford loan first disbursed on or after July 1, 2006, carries a fixed interest rate of 6.8 percent. The new rate on Parent Loans to University Students (PLUS loans) rose to 8.5 percent. Also, as of July 1, 2006, the interest rate on most new consolidated student loans is 7.14 percent, or 6.54 percent for borrowers in a grace period. Consolidated PLUS loans carry a 7.94 percent interest rate. Stafford loans first disbursed before July 1, 2006, still have variable rates. The interest rate is adjusted annually every July 1, and is capped at 8.25 percent.

Still, this interest rate scenario may or may not stay in force for a while. Democrats in Congress are promising to make student loan reform a key component of their social and economic agenda. And one of the pledges they've made is to drastically cut interest rates on

What's My Rate?		
	Disbursed before 07-01-06	Disbursed on or after 07-01-06
Stafford Loans	Variable Rate	6.8%
PLUS Loans	Variable Rate	8.5%
Consolidated Fed. Loans	Variable Rate	7.14 or 6.54%
Consolidated PLUS Loans	Variable Rate	7.94%

student loans. In fact, Democrats have introduced a measure to lower interest rates on Stafford loans by half—to 3.4 percent from 6.8 percent over a five-year period. If approved, and once it is fully phased in, the Democrats' measure would save the average college grad with $20,000 in student loans $4,420 over the life of his or her loans, according to estimates from the U.S. Public Interest Research Group Higher Education Project.

The Democrats' proposal to lower student loan interest rates passed in the House in early 2007 and, as of this writing, was slated to be voted upon in the Senate. While it remains to be seen what will happen on the legislative front with student loans, there are some things that we know have already changed.

Students from the class of 2006 will be the first crop of graduates who can shop around for lenders. This is a big advantage because in years past, college grads were stuck with whomever their original lender was. Now, each successive graduating class will be able to refinance their student loans with whatever lender they choose. This will give them the flexibility and power to seek out lenders that provide added benefits, such as cash rebates, lower rates for automatic deductions, or other sweeteners for making a specific number of on-time payments.

What Loans Are Eligible for Consolidation?

In order to qualify for direct consolidation loans, you must have at least one direct loan or Federal Family Education Loan (FFEL) Program

Lower Interest Rates on the Horizon?

If the Democrats have their way, here are the interest rates undergraduates will pay on new Stafford loans issued on or after July 1, 2007:

Loan Disbursement Date	Interest Rates
July 1, 2007	6.12%
July 1, 2008	5.44%
July 1, 2009	4.76%
July 1, 2010	4.08%
July 1, 2011	3.40%

The new rates would apply only to subsidized Stafford loans, which are received by 5.5 million students every year. Other federal loans and loans to graduate students would not be affected by the proposed measure.

loan that is in grace, repayment, deferment, or default status. If you are currently enrolled in school, you can no longer consolidate your loans. This is because your loans will be defined as having "in school" status, making those loans ineligible to be included in a direct consolidation loan. The Higher Education Reconciliation Act of 2005 eliminated the provision that allowed FFEL or direct loan borrowers enrolled in school at least half-time to request, with their lender's approval, the right to enter repayment early on Stafford loans. Consequently, repayment has been redefined as commencing six months and one day after the date you stop attending classes at least half-time. You can consolidate defaulted student loans—after first getting them into repayment status for three months or rehabilitating them for 9 to 12 months.

Some experts say the best time to consolidate is during a deferment or during the grace period before your loan is scheduled to be repaid. This way you'll get a better interest rate on your consolidated loan because federal loans provide for a lower interest rate while you're in school; as of early 2007, the rate is 6.54 percent. Once you start repaying the loan (after you graduate and go through your six-month grace period), your interest rate increases; currently it's 7.14 percent. Should you decide to consolidate, here are the some of the types of loans that are eligible for loan consolidation:

- Stafford loans (subsidized or unsubsidized)
- Perkins loans
- PLUS loans
- Health Professions Student Loans (HPSL)
- Health Education Assistance Loan (HEAL)
- Nursing Student Loan (NSL)
- National Direct Student Loan (NDSL)
- SLS Loan (formerly called ALAS Loans)
- Federal Insured Student Loan (FISL)

Remember: Federal Stafford loans are made to students while PLUS loans are made to parents through two loan programs:

1. The William D. Ford Federal Direct Loan Program, where you or your parents borrow directly from the federal government at participating schools. Direct loans include Direct Stafford loans, Direct PLUS loans, and direct consolidation loans; and
2. The Federal Family Education Loan (FFEL) Program, where private lenders provide federally guaranteed funds. FFELs include FFEL Stafford loans, FFEL PLUS loans, and FFEL consolidation loans.

WHO SHOULD CONSOLIDATE STUDENT LOANS—AND WHO SHOULDN'T

You may be wondering if it's in your best interest to consolidate your student loans. Well, experts say that you can benefit from a consolidation—to a greater or lesser extent—only by taking into account the full details of your personal situation. For those of you having serious difficulty making your monthly payments, you definitely should look at consolidation as one of the options that can give you some financial relief.

At the same time, you shouldn't automatically attempt to consolidate your loans if you could qualify for other, potentially more advantageous alternatives like a deferment, which would also lessen your economic burdens. Also, if you've already been paying off your student loans for many years, and are close to retiring that debt, it's not financially prudent to consolidate and get a loan that would stretch your payments out for a newly extended time period, causing you to pay additional interest charges unnecessarily.

"The average student carries about $20,000 in student loan debt. For someone just starting to earn a salary, or planning to continue their education, this number can be daunting, but it doesn't have to be a burden," says Kevin Walker, CEO of Boston-based SimpleTuition, Inc. (*www.simpletuition.com*), which helps students, parents, and others objectively compare education financing options.

Using the consolidation comparison tools on SimpleTuition's website, you can compare multiple financing options from a variety of lenders and sort your loan offers by monthly payment, total cost of the loan, number of payments, fees, and annual percentage rates. "A basic understanding of how and when to consolidate the loans can alleviate confusion and help lower payments from the start," says Walker.

Walker and other experts, like Robert Shireman of the Project on Student Debt, recommend that college grads not consolidate federal and private loans together. It's far better to consolidate those loans separately because federal and private loans have significantly different rates, terms, and fee structures. And by consolidating a government-backed loan with a private loan, you may lose some of the benefits afforded under the federal loan system.

One upside to cash-strapped borrowers is that consolidation can give you more flexibility. With standard federal loans, you're obligated to pay back your higher education debts in ten years. That can be tough if you're on a budget or your income is limited. Depending on the amount of money you owe, a consolidated loan affords you the chance to extend your repayment period to as long as 30 years.

FAQS ABOUT STUDENT LOAN CONSOLIDATION

How does loan consolidation work?
When you consolidate your student loans, your original debts are paid off and you roll the combined balances from your previous loans into one new, larger loan with a fixed interest rate.

What are the main benefits of loan consolidation?
It's easier to make one payment to a single lender. Your can lower your payments significantly by stretching out your repayment period. There are no fees, credit checks, or prepayment penalties. And the fixed interest rate is set by federal law, with a lifetime cap of 8.25 percent.

What are the main drawbacks to consolidating student loans?
Increasing the payment length results in substantially more interest charges over the life of the loan. You may lose cancellation, forgiveness, deferment, forbearance, grace-period, and other privileges on some loans. And once you consolidate your loans, your decision is permanent. You can't undo a loan consolidation.

How low will my monthly payments go if I consolidate my loan(s)?
It varies. But according to Student Aid Lending (*www.studentaid-lending.com*), which provides student loans nationwide, consolidating your student loans may reduce your monthly payments by as much as 54 percent. Just remember: up-front savings in the short-run translate into additional finance charges in the long-run due to longer repayment periods.

What will my interest rate be?

That depends on the interest rates you're presently paying on your student loans. The new interest rate on your consolidated loan will be a weighted average of all the interest rates you currently have, rounded up to the next nearest one-eighth of 1 percent. Under the law, federal consolidated loans also have a lifetime interest rate cap of 8.25 percent.

Are there fees associated with federal loan consolidation?

No. Consolidation is free. There are no application fees and no prepayment penalties.

Where can I get a consolidated loan?

To apply for an FFEL consolidation or a direct loan consolidation, contact the bank, lender, or credit union of your choosing via telephone or over the Web. Alternatively, if you don't have an FFEL lender in mind, call 1-800-433-3243 for help. Additionally, you can contact the Direct Loan Origination Center's Consolidation Department at 1-800-557-7392 or visit: *www.loanconsolidation.ed.gov.*

When you call to discuss your loan consolidation options, remember that private education loans are not eligible. And consolidation isn't just for students. PLUS loan borrowers (parent borrowers) can also consolidate their loans, provided the PLUS loans have been fully disbursed.

How can I get the best deal on a consolidated loan?

Because interest rates on federal consolidated loans are the same at every lender, getting the best deal boils down to choosing a lender with good service and one that offers a host of perks, such as interest-rate reductions after you've paid your loans on time for a fixed periods, such as 12 or 24 months. Some lenders also lower your rate if you agree to pay by automatic debit.

Maximize Your Grace Period—and Get the Lowest Consolidation Rate

If you want to consolidate your loans as soon as you graduate, it's possible to snag the lower grace period interest rate and still enjoy your full six-month grace period without making any payments.

The way to do this is to carefully fill out the federal consolidation loan application. On it, you'll find Section D, which contains a question that allows you to enter your grace period end date. If you write down a date on this section, your lender can't complete processing of your application or disburse your loan until that date.

As a result, you can apply for a consolidation loan at any point during your grace period, get the lower grace period interest rate, and still put off making payments until your six-month grace period ends.

What happens when I consolidate my loans during the grace period?

Some grads choose to consolidate their loans during their grace period in order to receive the grace rate on their loans, which is .60 percent below the rate you'll pay once you begin repaying your loans. In consolidating during the grace period, however, you automatically waive the remainder of your grace period and your loan payments are immediately due.

Is there a maximum or minimum loan limit for a federally consolidated loan?

No. There are no dollar limits on the amount of student loans you can consolidate.

If I've consolidated my loans already, can I get a new consolidation loan?

Yes, under certain conditions. You can include existing consolidation loans in new direct consolidation loans if you include at least one other FFEL loan or direct loan into your existing direct consolidation loan or your existing FFEL consolidation loan, or if you're attempting to consolidate an FFEL consolidation loan that's been submitted to a guaranty agency for default aversion by your loan holder.

How long does it take for a loan consolidation to be processed?

That depends on your lender, as well as the number and types of loans you presently have. But as a rough guide, plan on the process taking as much as six to eight weeks. Your first payment will then be due within 45 days after the consolidation is finished.

What is the difference between the FFEL program and the direct consolidation loan program?

The FFEL program involves bank-based loans and the direct consolidation loans are made through the Department of Education. According to the Department of Education's website, some differences between the programs may include:

- Minimum balances or numbers of loans required to apply
- Types of loans that can be consolidated
- A prior account relationship may be required
- Repayment incentive benefits to encourage good repayment behavior
- The convenience of electronic debit, ensuring that monthly payments are made on time
- Repayment plans offered, such as payments sensitive to a borrower's income, family size, and total education indebtedness

If your credit is shaky, you might have to go with a loan consolidation through the FFEL program. That's because with FFEL consolidation loans, no credit check is required, even for PLUS borrowers, who are typically parents of students in college. With direct loan consolidation, however, PLUS borrowers will be subjected to a credit check to make sure they don't have a negative credit history.

Before you settle on a loan consolidation program, use an online calculator or two that can tell you how much your consolidated loan will cost you in the long-run.

In the end, your best bet at getting a consolidation loan that fits your needs is to do your homework, and learn as much as possible from potential lenders about how your loan will be handled and what features or special benefits a prospective lender offers. It's only by becoming a savvy consumer, and making informed choices, that you'll wind up with student loans—whether consolidated or not—that you can live with comfortably.

7

PAY LATER

Savvy Ways to Put Off Making Payments

Now you know how to pay down those student loans, but what if you can't start now? In this chapter, we'll talk about smart strategies for postponing college debt payments.

The two foremost methods for delaying student loan payments are deferments and forbearances. It's important to distinguish between the two because they are very different mechanisms. A deferment is a suspension of your loan payments. You are automatically entitled to a deferment if you meet certain conditions. For example, deferment is mandatory if you earn less than the poverty line—right now that's $1,100 monthly or $13,200 a year for a family of two—or if your student loan payments exceed 20 percent of your income.

Forbearance is a temporary modification of your loan repayment schedule, resulting in student loan payments being suspended or reduced. Forbearance is granted at the lender's discretion; it isn't an automatic right for student loan borrowers.

In obtaining either a deferment or forbearance, you achieve the goal of halting those weighty student loan payments in the here and now. There are a host of reasons why you may not be willing or able to currently tackle your student loans. Some reasons might include:

- You don't have a job or you're underemployed.
- You have other high debts, like credit card bills or medical bills.
- You have a family to support.
- You simply don't *feel* like it. (Just kidding!)

In all seriousness, even though you may have a litany of reasons for not *wanting* to pay right now, in the eyes of the law and from your lender's perspective the only question that really matters is: are you legally entitled to put off your student loan payments? Fortunately, there are a multitude of conditions under which you can qualify for a loan deferment or forbearance, and would be perfectly justified in requesting a temporary halt from making your normal monthly payments.

The trick to suspending your student loan payments, therefore, lies in first knowing which set of circumstances or which activities on your part can make you eligible for such relief, and then understanding how to apply for a suspension of loan repayments when you do meet your lender's requirements. As with most things in the student loan universe, the rules aren't hard and fast. Eligibility may depend on when your loans were taken out, if you had previous loans, and what type of loan is involved.

ARE YOU ELIGIBLE FOR A LOAN DEFERMENT?

You are automatically entitled to a student loan deferment if you meet certain conditions, and if you do qualify, your normal monthly payments get suspended. The interest charges accruing on those student loans are either paid by the government or paid by you, the borrower; it just depends on the type of loan.

A deferment is generally granted up to three years for each type of deferment and there are a variety of qualifying circumstances. Most of you already know that if you continue your education, let's say by taking classes in a graduate program, you'll have in-school status, which is one way to defer your student loan payments. You can also obtain a deferment based on being unemployed. To qualify, though, you must have been registered with an employment agency and you must have made at least six attempts in six months to actually get a job. (In other words: no sitting around watching soap operas all day, and then asking for financial relief.)

There is also an economic hardship deferment for which you might qualify. If you are on public assistance—for instance, receiving food stamps or other government or state aid—you are eligible for a student loan deferment, and you meet the federal definition of truly experiencing economic hardship. Even if you are working full time, you may qualify for a student loan deferment on the basis of economic hardship. Full-time employment is considered working 30 hours a week or more, and to qualify for a hardship deferment even though you're working, your income must be below certain guidelines—essentially you can't earn above the poverty level for a family of two.

Also, if you are working full time and you have a high debt-to-income ratio, you might qualify for a hardship deferment. According to the Department of Education, their definition of having a high debt-to-income ratio means your monthly income minus your student loan debt is less than $2,420 dollars. If you do the math, you'll see that the government is using a formula where your income works out to be about 220 percent of that poverty guideline that I mentioned before, the $1,100 a month figure. So if you're earning less than $13,200 annually (with two people in your household), you are going to meet the criteria and will qualify for a deferment.

Poverty Guidelines

In order to determine your family size, count the children you have (as long as you provide more than half their support), then count anybody else living with you who also receives more than half their support from you. You are considered to provide "support" to someone, according to the federal definition, if you give or loan them money, pay for such things as their car, clothes, and food, or provide them with dental and medical care, housing, payment of college expenses, and the like. In the chart below, find the column that shows where you reside. Then look down to your family size to determine the poverty guideline applicable for you.

2006–07 Poverty Guidelines

Family Size	48 Contiguous States and DC	Alaska	Hawaii
1	$9,800	$12,250	$11,270
2	$13,200	$16,500	$15,180
3	$16,600	$20,750	$19,090
4	$20,000	$25,000	$23,000
5	$23,400	$29,250	$26,910
6	$26,800	$33,500	$30,820
7	$30,200	$37,750	$34,730
8	$33,600	$42,000	$38,640
For each additional person, add	3,400	4,250	3,910

Source: Department of Health and Human Services

But what about those of you working less than full time (i.e., below 30 hours a week)? Well, there are criteria for you as well. You are considered to have low income if you work less than 30 hours a week, and earn less than a given amount of money (again, a formula tied to the poverty guideline), and you may qualify for a deferment. In all cases, your eligibility is tied to such factors as the date your loans were taken out, if you had previous loans, and the type of loan involved. Clearly, though, if you are experiencing any financial difficulties whatsoever, or if you meet other qualifying conditions, do yourself a favor and seek a loan deferment.

Let's say you have a loan with Sallie Mae-and many of you no doubt do. Sallie Mae owns or manages roughly $150 billion worth of student

Poverty Guidelines for a Family of Two

State	Monthly Income	Annual Income
Alaska	$1,375	$16,500
Hawaii	$1,265	$15,180
All other states	$1,100	$13,200

Source: Dept. of Health and Human Services

loans for nearly ten million customers, making it the nation's largest provider of student loans. Originally started as a quasi-government agency, Sallie Mae went private in 1997 and now dominates the market for federal and private student loans—including consolidation loans—to college undergraduates, grad students, and parents.

According to Sallie Mae, there are nearly 20 qualifying circumstances that would make you able to postpone your student loan payments.

Deferments available through Sallie Mae include:

ACTION Program. Covers full time paid volunteer service with an organization participating in a program authorized under Title I of the Domestic Volunteer Act of 1973.

Economic Hardship. Covers a borrower who earns less than minimum wage or exceeds a federally defined debt-to-income ratio. Also covers borrowers who are receiving public assistance or who are serving in the Peace Corps.

Graduate Fellowship. Covers study under an eligible graduate fellowship program.

In-School (Student). Covers both full-time and half-time study at eligible schools.

Internship/Residency. Covers service in an internship program that is required to receive professional recognition needed to begin professional practice or service. Also covers service in a medical internship or residency training program that leads to a degree or certificate awarded by an institution of higher education, hospital, or a health care facility that offers postgraduate training.

Military. Covers active duty status in the U.S. Armed Forces.

National Oceanic and Atmospheric Corps. Covers active duty service in the National Oceanic and Atmospheric Administration Corps.

Parental Leave. Covers a borrower who is pregnant or caring for a newborn or newly adopted child. Borrowers cannot be working full time and must have been enrolled at least half time in school six months prior to beginning the deferment.

Peace Corps. Covers volunteer service under the Peace Corps Act.

Primary Care Physician. Covers practicing primary care physicians who completed an internship in one of the following specialties: osteopathic general practice, family practice, general internal medicine, preventive medicine, general pediatrics.

Public Health Service. Covers service as a full-time officer in the Commissioned Corps of Public Health of the U.S. Public Health Service.

Rehabilitation Training Program. Covers a qualified individual's participation in a rehabilitation training program.

Summer Bridge Extension. Covers summer months for students who are deferred through the end of the spring academic period and are planning to re-enroll for the fall academic period.

Tax-Exempt Organization Volunteer. Covers full-time paid volunteer service with a tax-exempt organization that the U.S. Department of Education has determined to be comparable to service as a Peace Corps or ACTION volunteer.

Teacher Shortage Area (Targeted Teacher). Covers full-time teaching in a public or nonprofit private elementary or secondary school located in a teacher shortage area as defined by the U.S. Department of Education.

Temporary Total Disability. Covers a period during which a borrower is temporarily totally disabled or unable to secure employment due to caring for a dependent or spouse who is temporarily totally disabled.

Unemployment. Covers individuals who are seeking, but unable to secure, employment in the United States. The borrower can be receiving unemployment benefits.

Working Mother. Covers mothers of preschool-age children when the mothers are entering or re-entering the workforce.

Source: SallieMae.com

Other lenders that have loaned you money via the federal student loan program have similar qualifications for loan deferments, so it behooves you to check with your lender if you are in need of postponing your monthly payments. If you find out that you are not, in fact, eligible for a deferment, all is not lost. There's still the possibility of you being granted forbearance, which is another tool at your disposal.

FIGHT FOR THAT FORBEARANCE

If you receive forbearance on your student loans, you must pay the interest charges on the loans, unlike with deferments. If you don't pay that interest before the end of the forbearance term, it gets capitalized and added to your loan repayment amount.

Forbearance is usually granted for up to one year at a time. While forbearance for a qualifying situation can last as long as three years, forbearance can technically be granted over and over without federal limitation on the cumulative amount of forbearances periods. Some qualifying circumstances include poor health and excessive loan debt (i.e., student loans in excess of 20 percent of your monthly income). You also can get forbearance based on military mobilization or a national emergency that might affect you as a borrower. So if you get called up to do battle as an enlistee for the government, if you are actively serving in the Army, Navy, Air Force, or Marines, then by all means, you are in fact eligible to get forbearance or a deferment.

Beyond the situations described above, at some point in your life you may simply experience a really bad cash crunch due to a host of extenuating circumstances. If you expect your financial woes to last for several months or more, it's worthwhile to just call up your lenders, tell them about your dilemma, and request forbearance. It's far better to plan ahead and postpone your obligation to repay your student loans than to be late on your college debt payments or possibly even fall into default. As with deferments, forbearance options abound. Each case is different, so it's ultimately up to you to demonstrate credibly to your lender that you're having financial difficulty and are in need of forbearance. In most cases, when you're having a legitimate economic issue in your life, a simple phone call to your lender where you succinctly and earnestly explain your situation is sufficient to get that much-needed forbearance.

ECONOMIC HARDSHIP CASES—AND HELP FROM AN OMBUDSMAN

I've already described certain scenarios under which you might be deemed as qualifying for a hardship deferment or forbearance. But what if you get nowhere trying to convince your lender to suspend, postpone, or reduce your monthly student loan payments? You may find a sympathetic ear—and a bit of help—with an advocate within the Department of Education.

Have you ever heard of the Federal Student Aid (FSA) Office of the Ombudsman? Probably not, but this is office was created in 1998 and is charged with helping students resolve issues and better communicate with their lenders and loan services. So if you have a problem that hasn't been resolved, you might also want to contact the ombudsman.

The FSA ombudsman is Debra Wiley. She and her staff field about 300 calls a week and they informally resolve complaints from student loan borrowers. They won't pay loans on your behalf, educate you about the basics of financial aid (which you should do on your own), or reverse a decision that's been rendered. But they will hear you out, investigate your case, and contact your lender or loan servicer on your behalf if they feel your grievances are justified. If they believe your complaints lack merit, they'll be honest enough to tell you so, and will give you an explanation as to why they came to that conclusion.

The ombudsman's office also makes recommendations for improving service within FSA based in part on feedback they receive from student and parent borrowers. You can contact the FSA ombudsman online at *www.ombudsman.ed.gov*, via telephone at 1-877-557-2575, or through the mail at this address:

> U.S. Department of Education
> FSA Ombudsman
> 830 First Street, NE
> Fourth Floor
> Washington, DC 20202-5144

Before you ask for help, be sure you've done everything you can do to resolve your problem. (The ombudsman's website even has a checklist of what you should do before contacting their office.) If you do reach out to the ombudsman, don't expect this individual to wave a magic wand and make your lender see everything your way. Remember: this is a neutral, third party we're talking about (even though this office was set up by the Department of Education as a free service for borrowers). Still, the ombudsman may be instrumental in helping you move past issues where you and your lender are at an impasse.

The ombudsman can also tell you about options you may not have considered, depending on your loans' type and the particulars of your situation. The ombudsman's office doesn't handle complaints involving private loans, nor will it get involved in cases where the Department of Education has already begun formal legal actions against you.

With the variety of payment plans available, a host of payment postponement options, not to mention loan assistance repayment programs and help from other sources such as the FSA ombudsman's office, it's ludicrous to let your student loans slip into default—or stay there if they're already in default status.

As you've learned in previous chapters, some student loan repayment plans only require you to pay $5 a month—hardly an exorbitant sum, no matter what your income. For those of you experiencing severe financial difficulties due to unemployment or other circumstances, alternatives exist for you also through deferments or forbearance. You simply have to know what your options are, find out what type of relief you qualify for, and then reach out to your lender or loan servicer for help. Hopefully, no matter what your personal difficulties may be, you now are armed with the information and strategies you need to make sure you can handle your student loan debts from this point on.

For college grads of all ages, the goal is to manage those student loans effectively while you're in the repayment phase, and then pay them off completely as quickly as you're able to do so. It's only by implementing a carefully crafted plan of eliminating your college debt that you'll go from being buried in student loans to financially free. But if you had the wherewithal to make it through two years, four years, or maybe even eight years of schooling to get a higher education—a rigorous process in which most students actually drop out—you can also beat your student loan debt!

In the next chapter, we will look at how to clean up defaulted student loans. If you're in default, don't despair. There are solutions!

CHAPTER

CLEAN UP DEFAULTED STUDENT LOANS
How to Bring Overdue Accounts Current

If you have a student loan that is in default, you're probably pretty concerned about how to get out of this jam. Well, after reading this chapter, you'll know exactly what to do and you'll have all the information you need to turn that problem debt into one in good standing. To begin with, let's clarify what it means to have a loan in default as opposed to having a loan that is merely delinquent, or past due.

When your student loan payment is due, you likely will receive a notice from your lender or servicer telling you what amount to pay and where to send the check. If you don't make a timely payment, that student loan is immediately considered delinquent. Your payment could be due on the 15th and if it's not made, by the 16th, technically your loan is delinquent, or past its due date.

Some time will go by, and your lender or servicer will again start sending you notices. Sometimes the letter will come from the school itself. It depends on the loan type and the holder of the promissory note. But under current law, a default occurs on your student loan any time you have not paid what was due for 270 days. In some cases, a loan default comes after 330 days of missed payments. Keep in

113

mind that this 270 to 330 period comes after your six to nine month grace period, when you've graduated, left school, or dropped below half-time enrollment status.

So a defaulted student loan, unlike a merely delinquent loan, has really been overdue for quite some time.

How do you know whether the 270-day or the 330-day delinquency triggers a default? It depends on how you were supposed to repay your debt. If you have any type of Federal Family Education Loan (FFEL) loan that's been authorized under Section 435(i) Title IV of the Higher Education Act, a default occurs on an FFEL loan after a delinquency has persisted for 270 days for a loan with monthly repayment terms. If your loan was supposed to be payable in installments less frequent than monthly, then the 330-day delinquency is what triggers a default. This applies to loans that first went delinquent on or after October 7, 1998.

If, after making numerous attempts to contact you and get you to pay up, the lender is unsuccessful, it will typically put the loan in default and turn it over to the guaranty agency in your state. When you are declared in default on your student loan, and the maturity date of that promissory note that you signed gets accelerated, you trigger a clause in your loan provision agreement that basically says all the money is due immediately. This includes the principal and interest due on the loan.

Obviously a default has very negative consequences for you. But you may not be aware of all the ramifications, so it's important that you know what could happen. One penalty of being in default is that you are no longer eligible for any type of deferment or forbearance, which are two key payment-postponement methods used by people unable to pay those loans. You lose eligibility for other federal loans backed by the Federal Housing Authority or the VA. You also have very harmful consequences with regard to your credit report. And once your loan is turned over to a state guaranty agency or the federal Department of Education for collection, legally, any of the following things can happen:

- You likely won't be able to get an academic transcript or records from your school.

- You won't be able to get any more student loans.
- Your federal tax refund check may be withheld to repay your loan.
- You may have to pay extra collection costs to a private collection agency—as much as 25 percent extra, on top of the principal and interest that you owe.
- Your wages can be garnished, requiring your employer to forward anywhere from 10 to 15 percent of your disposable pay to the Department of Education to pay off your student loan.
- The Department of Education can sue you or take other legal actions against you.
- Your default will be reported to the credit bureaus, severely damaging your credit score.

Clearly, these are all very unpleasant outcomes, to say the least. But I want to draw your attention to the credit ramifications of having student loans. And then I want to discuss one particularly onerous aspect of the student loan system for anyone in debt.

STUDENT LOANS AND YOUR CREDIT REPORT

In Part 3, I discuss credit and the importance of a healthy credit report at length. Here, I want to note that student loans, like a mortgage, are a form of good debt. So banks and other lenders reviewing your credit report won't hold it against you that you've gone to school, earned a degree, and accumulated $10,000, $50,000, or even $100,000 worth of student loan debt in the process—as long as you are paying it on time.

Student loans are not something negative that hurts your FICO score or diminishes your potential to obtain bank loans, credit cards, mortgages, or other financing. The problem comes in, however, if you default on one of those student loans. That does negatively affect your credit standing, and it does so in a number of ways.

You may already know that any negative information about your bill payment history (such as a late payment) can be kept on your credit report for seven years at a minimum; ten years for a bankruptcy. But there is another provision in the law though under the Higher Education Act that toughens the severity of any negative information contained in your credit report. In essence, there are statues of limitation when it came to you being legally obligated to repay a debt and that creditor being able to sue you. In most states, for example, the statute of limitations on credit card debts range from three to ten years.

With a student loan, however, there is no statute of limitations of any kind. This means that if your student loan has defaulted and been turned over to a guarantee agency or the Department of Education, they can report your default forever on your credit report. Moreover, they have the right to file a lawsuit against you, get a judgment against you, garnish your wages, or take other legal actions against you—regardless of how long ago that debt was incurred. It could have been 5 years, 10 years, or even 25 years ago when you got those student loans.

The fact that creditors can "pursue you to the grave" over your old student loans, says Deanne Loonin, staff attorney at the Washington, D.C.-based National Consumer Law Center, gives the Department of Education tremendous power and puts you at an enormous disadvantage. The lack of a statute of limitations for student loans puts borrowers "in unenviable, rarified company with murderers, traitors, and only a few violators of civil laws. Even rapists are not in this category since there is a statute of limitations for rape prosecutions, at least in federal law," said Loonin in a 2006 report called *No Way Out: Student Loans, Financial Distress, and the Need for Policy Reform.*

The permanence of student loan debt is not the only challenge you'll confront with a defaulted loan. When you have to pay the additional collection costs tacked onto a defaulted loan, it is not a small sum of money by any stretch of the imagination. The Department of Education allows for their contractors to be paid up to 25 percent more than the initial principal and interest that you incurred as a borrower. In other words, you are going to pay what they call a contingent fee, which is the collection agent's commission.

When you start repaying your defaulted loan, you pay the commission first, then you repay the interest on the loan, then you repay your principal. So, again, imagine how much all of that can add up if you let it go on year after year. So you definitely do not want to be in a default situation.

For those of you who may have tried to get transcripts released, either because you wanted to go to graduate school or just wanted to have to a record of your grades, you probably know that your school may also refuse to release your transcript if your student loans are in default. Interestingly, there is no federal law that says that they can do this. However, each college campus may have its own institutional policy on this issue. And more often than not, the policy prohibits a student from getting a transcript released when the school has been notified by a guaranty agency or by the Department of Education that the student's loan is in default.

WAGE GARNISHMENTS

Defaulted student loans make you subject to wage garnishments, another of the fierce tools available to the hands of the Department of Education. But let me explain this process in a bit more detail because it is very different than a traditional wage garnishment. The kind of garnishment that the Department of Education can do is called an *administrative* wage garnishment.

This means they do not have to go to court, as do other creditors, in order to get a judgment against you from a court of law. With an administrative wage garnishment, an order is simply sent to your employer, requiring your employer to forward money right out of your paycheck to repay your student loan. The garnishment amount ranges from 10 to 15 percent of your disposable pay. So clearly, all of these negative consequences suggest that you do not want to be in a defaulted loan situation. It's worth you going to great lengths and doing everything in your power to prevent a default or get a defaulted loan out of default status.

Help! My Wages Have Been Garnished

As I previously explained, your student loans aren't subject to a statute of limitations, as are other forms of debt, like credit cards. So if you owe, ultimately you have to pay up or risk nasty things like wage garnishments. Not only is that a hugely embarrassing, and potentially career-damaging thing to happen to you at work, but a wage garnishment can put a serious crimp in your already tight budget.

Under the law, if the Department of Education pursues an administrative wage garnishment against you, the department can require your employer to turn over 10 percent of your disposable pay to be diverted in order to pay off your past-due student loan debt. This is all done without so much as a court hearing or a judgment against you. In fact, federal regulations require guaranty agencies to initiate wage garnishments as a means of enforcing defaulted loans.

The Debt Collection Improvement Act of 1996 authorized federal agencies, including the Department of Education, to garnish up to 15 percent of a debtor's disposable pay. So can anything be done about it? Actually, yes. You can fight the wage garnishment and demonstrate why it is that you can't afford that the payments and wage garnishment your lender or guaranty agency is seeking.

You'll build your case based upon various factors, such as your high day-care costs, your large credit card bills, your medical bills, and so forth. You then offer a counterproposal saying what amount you can afford to pay to the Education Department. All you need to do is fill out a three-page form to get the process started. This form is called a Financial Disclosure Statement, and it's designed especially for wage garnishment cases. Track down a copy of this statement on the Internet by visiting the Department of Education online at *www. ed.gov/offices/OSFAP/DCS/forms/fs.pdf.*

Do yourself a favor and follow the instructions on this form to the letter. For instance, fill in all lines that request dollar values or other information. If your answer to something is zero, don't just leave the line blank. Insert a zero (0). Also, provide written proof for all the statements you make on the form. If you say your credit card bills are $500 a month, give a copy of your Visa and MasterCard statements. And above all, if you claim any kind of financial hardship due to having kids, or child-care costs, you absolutely *must* submit a supplemental form called Declaration of Caregiver Services. This form needs to be filled out by the person who provides day-care for your children. That person will have to attest—under penalty of law—that he or she cares for your kids, and that you pay him or her X amount of money on a weekly or monthly basis. Without this important document, all your claims for child-care expenses will be disallowed, so don't forget to submit this form too.

The three-page Financial Disclosure Statement is slightly different than the Statement of Financial Status you submit to the Department of Education to propose a reduced monthly payment that you can afford. But both ask for detailed information about your income and expenses. And both require that you fully document and substantiate all the information you present. For instance, if you say that your rent is $1,200 a month, you should send a copy of your renter's contract or provide the front and back sides of your cancelled checks proving the amount of rent you've been paying for the past several months.

To get the feds off your back in a wage garnishment proceeding, you'll have to be meticulous in your documentation. Don't just send a letter with a sad sob story about how you've fallen on hard times lately. Back up everything you say with cold, hard numbers and written, irrefutable documentation so they know your story is legitimate. Send the Financial Disclosure Statement to:

U.S. Department of Education
PO Box 617763
Chicago, IL 60661-7763

When a guaranty agency or the Department of Education evaluates your case, they can use any method they want to determine the validity and relevance of your declarations. Some lending institutions and guaranty agencies rely heavily or even exclusively on your Financial Disclosure Statement. Others, including the Department of Education, rely on an analysis of your situation based on the standards used by the IRS when it evaluates Offers in Compromise proposed by debtors who can't pay their taxes.

In a nutshell, with this IRS-based standards approach, the Department of Education takes a look at your income and expenses, compares them against regional and national averages (obtained from Census Bureau data and other sources), then makes a determination as to whether or not a wage garnishment would cause severe financial hardship to you and your family. How convincing is your argument and how thoroughly can you back up your claims?

Why do I feel this is the critical, determining factor in the outcome of any hardship case presented before the Department of Education? Because they say so, in so many words, right in one of their most recent rule books on the matter. In the October 2004 Department of Education publication called *Options for Financially Challenged Borrowers in Default*, it states: "A debtor who claims to need to spend more for a particular kind of expense than the average amount spent by families in his or her cohort of the standards bears the burden of persuasion that the added amount is necessary."

This publication, by the way, is a must-read for any of you dealing with defaulted student loans or wage garnishment issues. The booklet comes from the U.S. Department of Education's Borrower Services Collections Group. It discusses the payment terms, refinancing options, and administrative discharge relief available to financially burdened college grads. I bet no one ever told you about it, right? Well, now you can review it for yourself at *www.ed.gov/offices/OSFAP/ DCS/forms/2004.Borrower.Options.pdf.*

What to Do If You Receive a Wage Garnishment Notice

If you do get a dreaded notice of a wage garnishment in the mail, don't panic and run off to Guatemala. Instead, face the issue head on and decide how you want to proceed. You basically have three options: (1) Pay the amount they ask; (2) pay a reduced amount; or (3) don't pay at all.

If you want to repay what you owe—and not claim a financial hardship—the Department of Education will set up an installment plan with you whereby you pay 15 percent of your disposable pay. You won't have to go through some big production proving your expenses. Just giving two recent paycheck stubs will be sufficient to establish your income. The wage garnishment won't begin, and the monthly payments—at exactly the same rate that would be allowed under the law with a garnishment—will begin. The difference is that this matter will be handled quietly, more or less, between you, your lender or guarantor, and the Department of Education. You'll save yourself the personal embarrassment and credit woes that come along with having a wage garnishment. You'll also preserve your professional reputation at work by heading this matter off before your employer is forced to get involved. Call the customer service department at the Department of Education at 1-800-621-3115 to start the process of arranging a voluntary repayment.

If you do want to claim a financial hardship status, and because of your current financial predicament you want to pay less than the garnishment amount shown on your notice, here's how to approach things. After you get a letter in which the Department of Education says it intends to garnish your wages, you should immediately obtain, fill out completely, and submit the Statement of Financial Status that I described earlier. Provide rock-solid proof of all your income and expenses. Give them two pay stubs, along with the last two years' W-2 statements and income tax filings. The department will then review your situation, analyze your income and expenses, and using the standards approach I previously explained, the agency will accept an installment amount based on your available income after necessary household expenses.

And guess what happens if it's determined that you're flat broke and you have no money left over after you pay all your monthly necessities? Believe it or not, you don't have to pay anything! Don't just take my word for it. Again, this is what their own rule book says, right on page 23: "If no amount appears available after expenses are met, the department suspends attempts to garnish." Does this mean you're off the hook forever and that you no longer owe your past-due student loans? Of course not; that would be too good to be true. The Department of Education has the right to—and will—check back in with you later to see if your financial situation has changed. "Any repayment agreement or suspension of enforcement action is subject to re-evaluation periodically, typically at six-month intervals," the rule book says.

If you object to a garnishment on hardship grounds or on another basis, you have to fill out and send in to the Department of Education a four-page form called an Administrative Wage Garnishment Request for Hearing in order to have your objection heard. You can find the form online at *www.ed.gov/offices/OSFAP/DCS/forms/Request.For.Hearing. pdf.* After you complete it in its entirety, send the form to:

U.S. Department of Education
PO Box 617763
Chicago, IL 60661-7763

You must choose to make your case to a hearing official via one of three methods. You can:

1. Submit written documents in support of your hardship claim;
2. Go to one of three Department of Education offices and present your case in person; or
3. Request a hearing over the telephone.

Before the hearing, you must also submit the Financial Disclosure Statement or another financial disclosure form of your choosing that details your income, expenses, and so forth.

If you want to make your case face-to-face, unfortunately you have to pay your own way to go to one of three offices in Atlanta, Georgia, Chicago, Illinois, or San Francisco, California. Most of you obviously won't do that—unless you just happen to live in one of those areas and for some reason feel you can more passionately argue the merits of your case in public as opposed to over the telephone or in writing. For a telephone hearing, provide the department with your phone number and let them know, using the Request for Hearing form, what time you are available Monday through Friday between 8 AM and 4 PM. They'll contact you to set up the hearing.

If you don't specifically ask for an in-person or telephone hearing, it's automatically assumed that you want an evaluation of your case based on the written evidence and documentation you supply.

The department will use the standards method in the hearing process to evaluate your claim of financial hardship. After the hearing, the department will notify you of its decision. One of three things can happen at this point:

1. The wage garnishment can stand as is. If you've done your homework, followed the tips I suggested, and aren't wasting their time and yours, this should be a highly unlikely outcome.
2. The hearing officer could reduce the amount of your wage garnishment. Under the law, this person has the power to order a lesser withholding amount, one that he or she deems appropriate based on a review of your case.
3. The hearing officer could decide to halt garnishment activity altogether, ruling that it would, in fact, create an undue hardship for you and your family.

Before you jump for joy at this last prospect, remember: the suspension of enforcement activity doesn't preclude the Department of Education from later demanding payment if and when your economic circumstances change. Interestingly, however, if you should experience a chronic financial crisis—and I'm talking year after year after year of being broke—it is possible that the Department of Education could cease collection activity against you. Under what circumstances, you ask, could this happen? The answer is: only in the extremely rare case in which the Department determines, after constant review, that the cost of hunting you down and trying to get you to repay either isn't worth the cost or doesn't serve the public's interest. This is obviously a highly rare event—so don't count on it!

WHO'S IN DEFAULT AND WHY?

Personally, I think it's a shame that so many people slip into default, especially in situations where it could have been readily prevented if only the borrower knew his or her options. In other cases, student loan defaults could be staved off if only school officials did more to help those who are at risk of having their student loans go into default because, believe it or not, there is plenty of evidence out there that suggests clear patterns of who is more apt to default on a student loan and who is not.

Here's the skinny: According to a survey by the Texas Guaranty Loan Agency, you're more likely to default on a student loan if you:

- Drop out of school.
- Work in a job different from your area of study.
- Don't know about your loan repayment options.

Borrowers who do not finish their degrees are ten times more likely to default on their student loans than people who leave school with a diploma. Drop-outs are also twice as likely to go into default on a student loan as unemployed people, according to a May 2005 report called *Borrowers Who Drop Out: A Neglected Aspect of the College Student Loan Trend*, by Lawrence Gladieux and Laura Pern of the National Center for Public Policy and Higher Education.

When you think about it, these "at risk" categories make sense.

The person who drops out of school doesn't earn a degree. That means his or her job prospects are generally far more limited than the person with a degree. Without a college diploma, the drop-out may have to take a lower-paying job, leading to difficulty in repaying student loans.

Also, consider the plight of those working in fields different from what they studied in school. You can imagine that many of these individuals tried initially to get jobs in their industry in a bid to leverage their degrees and put their higher education to use. But maybe the job market was flooded with applicants. Maybe there was an economic downturn. Maybe the jobs in their field dried up. Or maybe they got into the workforce and found out that what they studied in school didn't fulfill them professionally.

For whatever reason, these graduates ultimately accepted positions outside their area of study. Chances are, these jobs also were lower-paying than what the college grads could have or hoped to earn working in the areas that they studied in school. The net result is the same: financial difficulties led them to become delinquent in their student loans.

Equally frustrating is what happens to college grads who, because of a lack of information, fall into default when they were actually qualified for other forms of relief, like deferments, forbearances, or possibly loan forgiveness. The problem, however, is that students aren't really schooled in the intricacies of the student loan system. Upon graduation, or when students leave school, most people sit through that 10 or 15 minutes worth of "exit counseling" with their eyes practically glazed over.

Sometimes, human nature is to just try to avoid a problem and not deal with it. So when you started getting all those notices from your lender, and you knew you couldn't pay, I understand why you stuck your head in the sand and refused to confront your student loan dilemma. But the real question is: are you truly prepared to deal with the issue now? If you are, then you can readily resolve this crisis. It starts by making one simple phone call.

WHAT TO DO AND WHAT NOT TO SAY

By now, I'm sure you just want to know: Who do I have to call, and what can I do to fix things? Fortunately, you have several options. You'll also be glad to know that some recent changes in the law have actually made it easier than ever to get out of default. In a nutshell, to get out of default, you have four alternatives:

1. Consolidate the loan.
2. Enter a loan rehabilitation program.
3. Pay the loan off completely.
4. Get the loan discharged or cancelled.

Most borrowers will go for the first two options, for obvious reasons. The last two are discussed in Chapters 5 and 9, respectively. If you had the money, you almost certainly would have paid by now, so paying off the loan isn't realistic for the majority of college grads. Getting a discharge is very rare, though it can be done. Loan discharges or cancellations are generally granted for three reasons:

1. The death of the borrower or student;
2. The total and permanent disability of the borrower or student; or
3. The closing of the school you attended.

Before we look at loan consolidation and rehabilitation, and explore discharges and cancellations in depth in future chapters, it's important that you know what *not* to say when you first pick up the phone, call the Department of Education or your guaranty agency, and start dealing with your defaulted loans.

The following are various circumstances and reasons that will *not* be accepted as valid excuses for nonpayment of a student loan:

- "I moved or I was never sent a bill." Here's what the Department of Education will say in response: too bad. The notices they send are, in their language, a "convenience." It's your responsibility to provide your current address and to pay your bill regardless of whether or not you got a bill.

- "The quality of the instructors or facilities at my school were poor and I didn't get my money's worth." Once again, their attitude will be: so what? It was your responsibility to check it out beforehand. (Some rare exceptions do exist. See the later section on loan cancellations/discharges pertaining to school closings or fraud by a school.)

- "The statue of limitations in my state for collecting a debt has run out." That may be the case for other debts. But a special section of federal law (Section 484A[a] of the Higher Education Act) provides for no statute of limitations whatsoever on defaulted student loans.

- "I wasn't 18 or of legal age when I signed for the loan." Your young age (or youthful ignorance) doesn't matter. The argument you're trying to put forth is known as the so-called defense of infancy. But just because you were a minor doesn't mean that you didn't obligate yourself when you signed that promissory note, which is a binding contract. This is because no defense of infancy is accepted under the Higher Education Act of 1965.

- "I want a deferment or forbearance, and I qualify for one." Not so fast. You might *think* you're eligible for a deferment or forbearance, and under other circumstances you might be. Unfortunately, though, once you let your loan go into default you gave up your right to a deferment or forbearance. These options are only available *before* you default on a loan, or *after* a defaulted loan has been "cured" via loan rehabilitation and taken out of default status.

CONSOLIDATE YOUR LOANS

The quickest, easiest way to get out of default is to consolidate your loans. Federal loan consolidation is not available for private, or so-called alternative loans, only for federal loans. There are two federal loan consolidation programs: FFEL consolidation and direct consolidation loans.

Under the consolidation process, your existing loans are paid off and a new loan takes it place. Millions of people consolidate their loans every year, and many of them do it simply to avoid the hassle writing multiple checks each month to a variety of lenders. As discussed in Chapter 6, loan consolidation is convenient because all your loans get rolled up into one new, big loan and then you pay off that single debt.

As you might expect, though, consolidation has its price. Sure you might drop your payment from $700 a month to $250 a month through loan consolidation, but the catch is you'll wind up paying a lot more money in interest charges, and it'll take you far longer to get rid of your student loan debts. Still, if you need immediate relief this can be a worthwhile option to consider.

To get a loan consolidation after you've been in default, you must first show the government that you're ready, willing, and able to begin making regular payments. Under guidelines issued by the Department of Education, in order to receive an FFEL consolidation loan, you must get your defaulted loan back into repayment status. You can do this in only 90 days. Once you make just three on-time, full monthly payments in an amount that you and your lender agree upon, your defaulted loan is eligible for consolidation.

Under the terms of this program, a commercial lender then pays off your old student loan debt and issues you a new loan, along with a fresh promissory note, new interest rate, and an updated repayment schedule. Depending on how much you owe, the repayment period can be stretched out as much as 30 years.

After you've successfully made those three agreed-upon payments, your credit report is then updated, showing that your old loan has been paid off and now has a zero balance. Beware, however, that the old default notation will still remain on your credit report for seven years, and that doesn't look good to lenders. It's just that the default will be stated as paid in full.

The only way to get the default completely removed from your credit report is to go through the longer loan rehabilitation process, where you make 9 monthly payments on FFEL and direct loans, or 12 monthly payments on Perkins loans. This, in my opinion, is the preferred route, as it will help you restore your credit in a big way and that past default won't haunt you for years to come.

But what if can't get a loan consolidation with an FFEL consolidation lender? Don't worry. All is not lost. There's still the direct consolidation loan option. Even if you never had any direct loans, you can qualify for a direct consolidation loan if:

- You include at least one FFEL loan in your consolidation loan; and
- You were unable to secure a federal consolidation loan or weren't able to obtain a federal consolidation loan with income-sensitive repayment terms you could afford.

With the direct consolidation loan program, you can consolidate most defaulted FFEL and direct loan program loans, provided that you made "satisfactory repayment arrangements" with your current loan holder(s), which means that you made three payments in whatever amounts you and the lender agreed to, or you agree to repay your new direct consolidation loan under the income contingent repayment plan.

One big drawback to consolidating a defaulted student loan is that you won't just get away with paying the principal and interest on your loan(s). The Department of Education may tack on as much as 18.5 percent on top of what you owed to cover collection costs. Take that into consideration as you weigh this option, because it will certainly add to the length of time and the dollar amount you must fork over in order to pay off a consolidated loan.

To find out if you qualify for loan consolidation, contact the Federal Direct Consolidation Loan Info Center at 1-800-557-7392 or go online to *www.ed.gov/offices/OPE/DirectLoan*. The staff there should be able to tell you what your monthly payment will need to be for those three months while your loan is in repayment. Lenders like Sallie

Mae (*www.salliemae.com* or 1-800-524-9100) may also give you some guidance in this matter. To apply via the Internet for loan consolidation, go online to *loanconsolidation.ed.gov.*

Before you make a decision about consolidation, be sure to also read Chapter 6. It offers a slew of tips and advice about consolidation, including under what circumstances you shouldn't consolidate your loans, and which types of loans you shouldn't consolidate.

LOAN REHABILITATION PROGRAMS

As an alternative to loan consolidation, you can begin making payments on that old student loan debt. If you can't afford your regularly scheduled payments, you will be able to enter a loan rehabilitation program. Loan rehabilitation is available for most loans, including FFEL, federal Stafford loans, and federal PLUS loans. Defaulted loans in this category have likely been placed with a state guaranty agency. If you had a direct loan that went into default, then those loans are sent right to the Department of Education's debt collection services. If you had a Perkins loan, it could have either remained with the school or been sent to the Department of Education for collection. By now you should've tracked down your loans to find out where they are. But as a reminder, you can call 1-800-4-FED-AID (1-800-433-3243) if you need help locating your defaulted loans.

To rehabilitate a defaulted loan, you previously had to make 12 consecutive, on-time payments in order to bring that loan out of default status. As of July 1, 2006, the rules governing loan rehabilitation softened a bit. Now you only need to make nine consecutive payments in any ten-month period to bring your loan out of default. Perkins loans require 12 months worth of payments.

Again, remember you don't even have to make your normal monthly payment, or what the lender originally said you should be paying. In loan rehabilitation, you get a chance to show what you can really afford to pay. You and the lender ultimately agree on what's fair and reasonable, and then your new payments begin.

Once you've gone through loan rehabilitation, and you've made your nine consecutive payments, your loan gets reinsured. You are then eligible to have the loan purchased by a lending institution. After rehabilitation, your loan not only gets taken out of default, but the Department of Education will notify all the credit bureaus that you've paid up. The negative information will even be completely deleted from your credit file. How's that for getting a fresh start?

At this point, you will continue repaying your loan over a set time period—specifically, you'll have about nine years worth of payments remaining. The problem with this part of loan rehabilitation is that you might have made payments that were reasonable and affordable during that 9- or 12-month period, but all of a sudden, once your loans are out of default status and you've completed the rehabilitation process, the loan gets thrown into the standard ten-year repayment cycle.

This could cause your payments to surge astronomically. So this is the time at which you should complete a Statement of Financial Status, submit it to the Department of Education, and request lower monthly payments. And here's the kicker: you tell the department what you can afford to pay. You show them your true monthly bills— like your rent, electricity food costs, child care, and so on. And then you demonstrate that, even though your lender may want $500 a month, you can only pay $50—or whatever amount is possible given your circumstance. I can't stress enough how big a lifesaver this strategy can be for someone struggling with student loan debt.

Unfortunately, one of the problems with the student loan universe is that critical alternatives like this—where you only pay what you can afford and don't have to worry about defaulting—are rarely told to college grads. Sometimes calling certain agencies does little to help if the workers there don't know how to point you in the right direction. Even finding information about these options on the Web is next to impossible. After much sleuthing and research, however, I located this handy three-page Statement of Financial Status on the Internet. Here's where you can get it yourself: *www.ed.gov/offices/OS-FAP/DCS/forms/fs.pic.pdf.*

Believe me, this one form could be the single most powerful document needed by millions of people trying to manage their student loan debts and keep their heads above water. For more info about this all-important form and this process of requesting lower monthly payments, please see the section on "Economic Hardship Cases" in Chapter 7. Also, the Department of Education can give you additional information on the loan rehabilitation program.

Finally, for more help dealing with defaulted student loans, there are three additional resources that may help you:

1. Your school's financial aid office may suggest alternatives.
2. The U.S. General Services Administration
   (*www.pueblo.gsa.gov*)
   Consumer Information Center
   S. James Consumer Information Center—6C
   PO Box 100
   Pueblo, CO 81002
   (Request two booklets: *Direct Student Loan Consolidation* and *Paying for College.*)
3. Federal Trade Commission's Public Reference Branch
   (*www.ftc.gov*)
   Room 130, 6th Street and Pennsylvania Avenue, NW
   Washington, DC 20580
   (Request a pamphlet titled *Knee Deep in Debt.*)

Remember, even though you may be frustrated with the student loan system, enraged about how high your payments are, or disheartened by the massive student loans you're now forced to repay, it's far better to channel those feelings into action. Starting today—not tomorrow or next month—do what you must to begin pulling that defaulted student loan back into good standing.

Even if it causes you some short-term distress, in the long-run, you'll be so glad that you got rid of this problem once and for all. You'll be back in everyone's good graces—your lender, loan servicer, guaranty agency, and the Department of Education will all be happy. Your school officials will be notified, and that's a big plus. Your credit standing will improve enormously. And best of all, you'll have peace of mind, because you'll be one step closer to getting those student loans off your back. Isn't achieving that financial freedom worth it?

9

ELIMINATE STUDENT LOANS WITH LOOPHOLES

Qualify for Loan Cancellation or Get Others to Pay

For a college grad with big student loans, it's probably the closest thing you can imagine to hitting the lottery: getting a discharge or cancellation of all your loans and making those debts instantly vanish. Unlike the lottery, you're not going to receive a million dollar prize. But if you can get a lender to agree to cancel or forgive $20,000, $50,000, or even $100,000 worth of student loans, wouldn't that feel like you hit the jackpot?

Well, here's the good news for anyone struggling with federal student loan debt: you can, in fact, have those enormous student loans completely wiped out by taking advantage of instances where you're already eligible for loan cancellation or forgiveness. Let's call these instances loopholes of the student loan world, because they represent narrow windows of opportunity that you take advantage of by escaping repayment of your student loans altogether.

And here's even better news: even if you're not eligible for loan cancellation, every single one of you reading this book can get up to $60,000 worth of your college debts paid off by the government, just by tapping into a little-known resource called the Federal Student

Loan Repayment Program. This program allows any federal agency in the country—and there are hundreds of federal agencies—to make payments on your behalf totaling as much as $10,000 a year to your loan holder. I think this rarely discussed option could be a lifesaver for many of you. So I'll give you all the details about the program in this chapter. This option isn't available to those of you who have private loans. But there's a solution for you as well, courtesy of your employer. I'll explain how later in this chapter.

Additionally, I'll highlight a host of other loan repayment assistance programs that you probably never knew existed. Some of them require you to volunteer with nonprofit groups or work off your debts by engaging in activities that promote various social or public goals; others are merely yours for the asking.

Lastly, I'll reveal a variety of other national initiatives, organizations, and mechanisms for getting your student loans repaid—without you actually paying a dime. These alternative measures, which essentially boil down to you using Other People's Money (OPM), can help you go from deep in debt to financially free.

LOAN CANCELLATION PROGRAMS— BIG HASSLES, EVEN BIGGER PAYOFF

Under federal law, you can get your student loans cancelled or discharged due to any of the following circumstances:

- Death
- Total and permanent disability
- School-related issues or improper certification by your school
- Full-time teaching or public service work
- Military service
- Bankruptcy

Before I explain the nuts and bolts of what's required for these various loan cancellations, let me first describe a multitude of scenarios that won't get you a loan discharge. If you dropped out of school for any reason, experienced personal problems that forced you to abandon your studies, didn't like your instructors, couldn't get a job after graduation, were plagued by financial difficulties, or even if you thought the quality of the instruction you received was subpar, you cannot get a discharge. None of those reasons will hold weight with the Department of Education. Let me also caution you that getting a student loan cancelled or discharged is rare and often requires tremendous perseverance, know-how, and work on your part.

Having said that, even though obtaining a discharge can be a big hassle, it is nevertheless certainly worth the effort and frustration you may experience in the process.

Discharges Due to Death

I can already guess what many of you are not thinking about getting a disability discharge for reasons of death. You're thinking, 1) I'm reading this book, Lynnette, so I'm obviously alive and not dead! and 2) I don't have any plans on dying anytime soon, nor do I *want* to die, so I'm sure a death discharge doesn't apply to me and can't benefit me.

Well, I believe you when you say you're alive—and trust me, I'm glad that you still have a pulse and the wherewithal to read this book and benefit from it! But just because you're still breathing doesn't mean you or someone you love can't benefit from a death-related disability discharge of your student loans.

Here's how: Federal law provides for discharge of student loans in the event of the death of the *borrower* or the death of the *student* for whom a parent obtained a PLUS loan. So let's say your mom took out a PLUS loan for you and unfortunately she later died. As a PLUS loan recipient, your mom was the borrower, not you. Even if you and she had an agreement by which you would actually pay back the loan, legally she's the one obligated to do so. Moreover, if your dad cosigned the application, he wouldn't have to pay the loan back either, as the law says that in the event of the student's death or the borrower's death, the obligation of the borrower and any endorser is discharged.

So here's the bottom line for any of you with parents who took out PLUS loans on your behalf: just know that the death discharge is available not just if *you* die, but if your *parents* pass away. By the same token, you should let your parents know that if *you* die, any PLUS loans *they* may be repaying can be cancelled.

Lastly, some of you may be married or may have previously consolidated student loans with your spouse when that was possible, under old federal rules. Let your partner know that in the event of your death, he or she doesn't have to continue paying off those old student loans. To secure a death discharge, you (or a loved one) have to apply for it. You'll need to get an original or certified copy of the death certificate and send it to the loan holder for Federal Family Education Loan (FFEL) or direct Stafford loans. For federal Perkins loans, the death certificate must be presented to the school(s) when you obtained your degree.

A Conditional Disability Discharge

If you were totally and permanently disabled in years past, you used to be able to get a letter from a doctor that testified to your condition and that supported your application to have your student loan debt completely discharged. Back in 2002, however, the Department of Education tightened the guidelines and the rules concerning those loans that were being discharged due to permanent and total disability. Essentially, the department said you can be deemed totally and permanently disabled only if:

- You can't earn a living due an injury or illness that is likely to persist indefinitely or that is likely to result in death;
- Your doctor certifies that you are 100 percent disabled based on the definition above; and

- You go through a conditional discharge period for three years, affirming over and over again that you really are disabled.

What all this means is that now, not only do you have to have the support of your doctor attesting to your total and permanent disability, you must also agree to be subjected to a three-year period of close monitoring and scrutiny by the Department of Education.

During this conditional discharge period, the department will check with the IRS and see whether or not you earn income. They'll have you attest, year after year for those three years, that you continue to meet the definition of being disabled. During this conditional period, you don't have to pay back the principal or interest on your student loans. If you continue to be deemed as totally and permanently disabled, at the end of the three-year conditional period your student loans will be cancelled. If, for some reason, you don't continue to meet the cancellation requirements, you must start repaying those college debts.

The department's definition of disability, by the way, is far stricter than even the Social Security Administration. The Department of Education says you're truly disabled only if you can't work or earn money because of a major injury or illness that is expected to continue indefinitely or that is likely to result in death. Again, your doctor has to also sign forms stating this as well.

Now I know some of you will say, "Good grief. I might have suffered an injury or illness that's temporary in nature, but I certainly don't think it'll last indefinitely, and I sure as heck hope it won't kill me!" Well, I hope that you're right. But here's where the rules get a little murkier. The Department of Education won't ban you from working altogether. In the fine print of the rules concerning disability discharges, you'll find that you are allowed to work—and remain eligible for that disability discharge—as long as you don't earn more than the poverty level, which is currently about $13,100 a year.

Based on all of this, I wouldn't blame you for thinking that a disability discharge is impossible to obtain. For a while, that's what

Jayne C. thought too. Jayne is a 38-year-old college graduate who lives in Philadelphia. As an undergrad she attended Temple University, got a degree in journalism, and later earned graduate degrees from Columbia University and the University of Pennsylvania. In pursuing her higher education goals, however, Jayne amassed student loans into the six-figure territory. Unfortunately, in 2003 Jayne suffered a host of maladies. She soon went out on disability from her job, and, after being declared by her doctor as totally and permanently disabled and unfit to work, Jayne applied with the Department of Education to have her student loans cancelled.

As of this writing, Jayne has been through her probation (i.e., the three-year conditional period), and has so far received a conditional discharge of all her outstanding student loans. The exact discharge amount totaled: $122,730.50; accrued interest to be capitalized was $728.31, resulting in a total of $123,458.81 worth of student loans being cancelled.

Getting that discharge, though, was a long and arduous process, Jayne warns. Multiple phone calls to her lender and loan servicer to inquire about disability discharges were exercises in frustration. Customer service representatives from Sallie Mae initially said they had no information about disability discharges, nor could they point Jayne in the right direction to find application forms online. "It's almost like a hidden secret that they don't want you to know about," says Jayne.

And that was only the first part of the battle. Her doctor was asked at least a half dozen times to fax documents that he'd already sent. The physician also had to reword his explanations about Jayne's condition to the department's satisfaction. "It got so bad that every time I would go see him, I would be carrying that form, and he would say: 'Oh this again,'" recalls Jayne.

One time Jayne's entire application was rejected merely because she'd put a line through a date on the form, and inserted the correct date. Despite all the hassles, Jayne knows it was worth it. According to her paperwork, in addition to her discharge amount of $123,458.81, the estimated amount of interest Jayne would've paid during the 30-year term of her loans would have been an additional $162,244.86, resulting in total payments of $285,703.67. "I would've been paying this for the rest of my life," she says.

Not all loan cancellations are as dramatic or as difficult to obtain as Jayne's.

Take the case of Jaclyn Ward, who went to Harvard College and then graduated from Fordham Law School in 2003. Now she works as an assistant district attorney in the Manhattan, New York, DA's office, a position that enables Ward, over a five-year period, to get $4,000 in undergraduate Perkins loans forgiven, and another $17,900 in law school loans discharged. Every year, Ward simply fills out a form indicating that she still works for the DA's office. "Not too difficult considering that I will get approximately $22,000 in tax-free loan forgiveness," she says.

"The most difficult part of the whole process was getting access to the knowledge," Ward adds. "I spent a lot of time investigating what options were open to me to help me with my loans. When I initially told Harvard that I was eligible for the Perkins forgiveness they told me I wasn't because I wasn't considered law enforcement. I had to do research and show them the congressional record where Congress deemed ADAs law enforcement officers. It's amazing how little financial aid officers know sometimes."

School-Related Discharges and False Certification

If the school that you attended closed before you could earn your degree, or if you withdrew from the school or were on an approved leave no more than 90 days before it closed, you can also qualify to get your student loans cancelled. Those of you who completed your studies elsewhere or by transferring academic credits from the closed school to another school are not eligible for this discharge.

The nice aspect about a closed-school discharge is that when a student loan debt is cancelled for this reason, you get a really sweet deal. For starters, you no longer owe anymore payments. Additionally, the government will actually give you money-by providing you with a refund for any student loan payments you made in the past in connection with a loan obtained at the closed school. Third, with any student loan that gets discharged, the servicing agency that has been handling your loan will notify all three of the credit bureaus that your loan was discharged. They, in turn, will delete any negative credit history, making you eligible to apply for federal student aid and get all the benefits that would be available to you if did not have any problems, such as a defaulted student loans. If you think your school closed and you need to check the date of the closure to determine your eligibility for a loan discharge, you can search the Closed School Database maintained at this website: *wdcrobcolp01. ed.gov/CFAPPS/FSA/closedschool/searchpage.cfm.*

A host of other school-related discharges also exist for student loan borrowers, and they fit under the umbrella of what's called false certification or improper certification. If you took out a direct loan or an FFEL on or after January 1, 1986, you might qualify for a false certification discharge if you (or your parents) received a loan that was falsely certified by an eligible school. According to the Department of Education, your eligibility to borrow is considered to have been falsely certified if any of the following conditions were met:

- The school admitted you on the basis of ability to benefit from its training, but you did not meet the applicable requirements for admission on the basis of ability to benefit.
- The school forged loan documents by signing your name without your permission on a loan application or promissory note.
- You had a physical, mental, or legal status or a condition at the time you enrolled in school that would've legally barred you from getting a job in your field of study. For example, you were imprisoned or had a conviction that prevented you from obtaining employment in your chosen area of study.

- You were the victim of identity theft. This new type of false certification discharge became effective July 1, 2006. As of this writing, discharge guidelines were still being developed. But in the meantime, the Department of Education says that you get forbearance and a halt to any collection activities if you show your lender or guaranty agency reasonably persuasive evidence that your loan may have been falsely certified as a result of a crime of identity theft.

Teaching and Other Service-Based Cancellations

Two other categories that you might qualify for with regard to getting your student loans discharged or cancelled pertain to service-based work. You can get your educational loans cancelled, or at least greatly offset, for jobs in teaching and public service. Teachers qualify for loan forgiveness in the amount of $5,000 or $17,500 under the Teacher Loan Forgiveness Program. The money is usually doled out to those who teach in low-income neighborhoods, those who teach certain math, science, and special education subjects, and individuals who work in places where there are critical shortages of qualified educators. Additionally, child-care providers, nurses, and others in the medical field who are helping individuals in impoverished areas or high-need communities can also qualify for loan discharges. So if you happen to be a doctor or nurse working in one of these areas, by all means investigate and see whether you qualify for a loan cancellation and in what amount.

Military Discharges

Effective October 7, 1998, all borrowers of Perkins loans are entitled to have those loans discharged if they served in the U.S. armed forces. This cancellation privileges applies to Perkins loan recipients regardless of when the loan was made or what the terms on the original promissory note are. Military personnel qualify for loan cancellations in an amount up to 50 percent of their Perkins loans if they serve in areas of hostility or regions of imminent danger.

Bankruptcy Discharges

Under federal law, as of October 8, 1998, you can no longer discharge student loan debt in a bankruptcy proceeding. As with most laws, however, there are loopholes and exceptions to the rule. In this case, it is technically legally possible to have your student loans discharged when you file for bankruptcy protection, but as a practical matter it is very, very difficult to get a judge to sign off on it. To have your student loans cancelled via bankruptcy, you have to prove to a judge that repaying your educational debt would cause you a substantial and undue hardship as defined by case law in your jurisdiction. Historically, most judges have been loathe to allow students to get rid of their student loans in bankruptcy court. Each claim is assessed on a case-by-case basis, and student loan discharges via bankruptcy are highly rare, even among those who've tried to demonstrate severe financial hardships.

WHAT TO DO IF YOUR DISCHARGE APPLICATION IS DENIED

I've already warned you about how difficult it can be to get a student loan discharged. Unfortunately, part of what's makes it tough is that for most discharges, the ultimate authority on the matter is the holder of your loan. The loan holder has the final power to say yes or no to your request for a discharge and you don't have the right to appeal the decision to the Department of Education, except in two instances: with false certification and forged signature discharges on FFEL and direct student loans. If your claim for a discharge for these types of loans is rejected, you can take your case to the department and ask officials there to review your denial.

Other than that, your best bet in handling a rejected application, if you truly feel you have a valid and worthy claim, is to be persistent in your pursuit of a discharge and to provide as much documentation to your lender as possible in support of your case. This may mean making multiple financial disclosures about your personal situation, explaining your argument time and time again to different people at your lender's office, or writing letters to supervisors or an ombudsman within a bank or lending institution.

Because the ultimate decision rests with the lender, that's the place you have to target your efforts. You should also try to find people who've been successful in getting the type of discharge you're seeking. Ask them for tips and tricks they learned along the way. That firsthand advice from someone who's been through what you have and received a hard-fought discharge could be just the prescription you need to turn a rejection into an approval.

LOAN FORGIVENESS PROGRAMS AND LOAN REPAYMENT INITIATIVES

Most loan forgiveness programs and loan repayment assistance plans can be grouped into four categories:

1. Loan forgiveness for teaching
2. Loan forgiveness for volunteers
3. Law school loan forgiveness
4. Medical school and health-care-related loan forgiveness

Loan Forgiveness for Teachers

Teaching is a great and honorable profession. You help to mold and shape young minds. You're educating the next generation. And you're a role model for hundreds of youth. Despite these facts, teachers often get scant respect. Nowhere is that more evident than in their paychecks. Well, despite the low salaries in the teaching profession, you can get a teaching gig that can help you pay off your loans, or more, accurately, one that will qualify you to have your loans forgiven.

Do this by teaching special education courses, teaching at a school that services low-income students, or teaching in a designated teacher-shortage area. The American Federation of Teachers maintains a list of other loan forgiveness programs for teachers at *www.aft.org/teachers/jft/loanforgiveness.htm*. You can also get more information about loan forgiveness options for teachers at FinAid (*finaid.org/loans/forgiveness.phtml*).

Loan Forgiveness for Volunteers

As a volunteer, you basically agree to swap your time and talents in the interest of the public good. And hey, there's nothing wrong with being a do-gooder—especially if it'll bail you out of those massive student loans. Here are some volunteer programs to check into in order to get student loan forgiveness:

AmeriCorps. You have to agree to devote a year of your life volunteering for AmeriCorps, and in exchange you'll get $4,725 to pay down your college debt, and a stipend of up to $7,400. AmeriCorps is administered by the Corporation for National Service. Here's how you can contact them:

> Corporation for National and Community Service
> 1201 New York Avenue NW
> Washington, DC 20525
> 1-800-94-ACORPS (1-800-942-2677)
> 1-202-606-5000
> Website: *www.americorps.org*
> E-mail: *Questions@americorps.org*

VISTA (Volunteers in Service to America). Vista focuses on community development and ending poverty, homelessness, and illiteracy in the United States. This organization will pay off $4,725 of your loans if you help them promote their cause for at least 1,700 hours. Call 1-800-942-2677 or log onto *www.friendsofvista.org*.

Law School Loan Forgiveness

The bad news is that you graduated with a ton of debt to get your law degree. The good news is that many law schools forgive the loans of students who serve in public interest or nonprofit positions. To find out how you can get your law school loans forgiven, start by reaching out to Equal Justice Works (*www.equaljusticeworks.org*), which was formerly called the National Association for Public Interest Law. All you college grads with law degrees should write or call Equal Justice (2120 L Street, NW, Suite 450, Washington, DC 20037-1541; phone 1-202-466-3686) and ask for a copy of the group's 48-page book called *Financing the Future: Responses to the Rising Debt of Law Students.* It's also available online at *www.equaljusticeworks.org/financing-the-future2006.pdf.*

Through that publication and others, you'll discover how law schools, states, and philanthropists are helping college grads, especially lawyers, pay back their student loans. The new trend is toward the development of so-called LRAPs: Loan Repayment Assistance Programs, as more and more conscientious members of society recognize that it's not in the public's best interest to have a whole generation of students awash in debt. It's especially harmful in the legal arena, because law school grads who can't pay their student loans can't take public interest (translate: lower-paying) jobs where they could help poor communities or those disenfranchised members of society who, without some assistance, would not have access to all their rights under the law. To show you how dire the situation is for law school grads, take a look at these statistics.

Equal Justice reports that:

- More than 80 percent of law school students use loans to pay for their law degree.
- For graduates of the class of 2005, the average amount borrowed in law school was $78,763 for those attending private schools and $51,056 for public school students.
- The median entry level salary for an attorney from the class of 2005 was $44,000 for state and local prosecutors; $43,000 for public defenders;

$40,000 for attorneys with public interest groups (like those dealing with immigrant or civil rights issues); and $36,000 for lawyers working at civil legal services organizations.

But promising signs are emerging that suggest law school grads will increasingly be getting relief. For instance, 100 law schools now have LRAPs, according to Equal Justice Works. Additionally, many state governments are creating their own Loan Repayment Assistance Programs for lawyers. In 2006, there were 17 state LRAPs in the United States, including Arizona, Florida, Indiana, Kentucky, Maine, Massachusetts, Minnesota, Missouri, Montana, New Hampshire, New Mexico, New York, North Carolina, Texas, Washington, and Washington, DC. Moreover, additional loan repayment assistance programs were being advocated for or developed in California, Georgia, Illinois, Iowa, Louisiana, Ohio, Oregon, Pennsylvania, and South Carolina.

If your employer needs help setting up an LRAP, you can also get a book from Equal Justice called *The LRAPs Training Workbook*. It's a step-by-step guide to improve an existing LRAP. The material is organized to take you through different stages of improving an LRAP. From the need for LRAPs to program design to funding, this workbook explains many of the issues involved in creating a successful program that benefits all parties involved.

The American Bar Association (ABA) has also created an important book that I highly recommend. It too gives detailed, step-by-step advice on this subject of LRAPs. The ABA's 77-page book is called *A Resource Guide for Creating State Loan Repayment Assistance Programs for Public Service Lawyers*.

Even if you just want to join in the effort, you can learn tips for how to help mobilize and support these kinds of efforts by tapping into the ABA's toolkit. It's located online at *www.abanet. org/legalservices/downloads/lrap/statelraptoolkit.pdf.*

Medical School and Health-care-Related Loan Forgiveness

Did you go to med school and wind up with student loans equal to some people's mortgages? Rest assured that you can get help knocking those education debts down. Here's a sampling of what's out there for doctors, nurses, occupational therapists, and others working in the healthcare field.

A little-known loan repayment program at the National Institutes of Health can provide eligible college grads with up to $35,000 a year if you have a PhD or MD and you work or research in the areas of general clinical medicine, pediatrics, fertility, or health disparities. Get more information at *www.lrp.nih.gov.*

The Nurses Reinvestment Act is a scholarship/loan repayment program that was authorized in the Public Health Services Act by the Department of Health and Human Services. It's aimed at nursing students who agree to serve in critical need areas after college graduation.

If you're a registered nurse, the Nursing Education Loan Repayment Program (NELRP) will pay anywhere from 60 to 85 percent of your student loans in exchange for work in areas experiencing a shortage of nurses. For more information, call NELRP at 1-866-813-3753 or visit *www.bhpr.hrsa.gov/nursing/loanrepay.htm.* You're not eligible to apply for this program if you are in default of any federal debt, like delinquent taxes or a defaulted student loan. Nurses in this the NELRP generally work in:

- Disproportionate share hospitals
- Nursing homes
- Federally designated health centers
- Federally designated migrant health centers
- Public health departments

- Rural health clinics
- Indian health service centers

The NELRP is a competitive program but well worth the effort, if you can get selected. And your chances of getting chosen are actually decent. According to its latest data, in 2005 NELRP received 4,465 eligible applications a made a total of 803 awards, with total obligated funds topping more than $19 million. I like those odds. This isn't like the lottery or something where you've got a 1 in 25 million chance of striking it rich. The numbers show that NELRP is generously funding roughly nearly one in five applicants.

Some groups offer forgiveness programs to physicians who agree to practice for a set number of years in areas that lack adequate medical care (including remote and/or economically depressed regions).

The Indian Health Service Loan Repayment Program permits health professionals to sign a contract, agreeing to work for a period of time in IHS health care facilities. In return, the IHS repays all or part of your debt for professional training and education. Get more info at *www.ihs.gov.*

Physicians, nurses, and dentists can agree to provide health care services for two to four years in areas of the country sorely lacking in qualified medical professionals and qualify for the National Health Services Corps Loan Repayment Program. The program offers scholarships and/or loan repayment programs, in addition to giving you a salary in exchange for using your medical talents in poor and underserved communities. For more info, call 1-916-654-1833 or visit the website of the Office of Statewide Health Planning and Community Development at *www.oshpd.cahwet.gov.*

Other Loan Forgiveness Programs

In addition to all these program-specific options, federal entities, and national organizations, your state or school might offer service-based programs that cancel, reduce, or repay part of your student loans.

Some examples include:

- Agriculture Education Loan Forgiveness Program
- New York Physicians Loan Forgiveness Program
- New York Social Work Loan Forgiveness Program
- Association of American Medical Colleges

Contact your state agency for postsecondary education to see what programs are available in your region. For the address and telephone number of your state agency, call the Federal Student Aid Information Center at 1-800-4-FED-AID (1-800-433-3243). You can also find this information at *www.studentaid.ed.gov.* At the site, click on the "Funding" tab, then go to "State Aid." Also check out loan forgiveness programs that may be available to you through trade groups, religious, civil, or professional organizations with which you are affiliated.

Lastly, for more info about loan forgiveness options, pick up a copy of *The Student Loan Forgiveness Directory* by the Fannie Mae Foundation and National College Scholarship Foundation. The book contains a list of some 200 institutional loan forgiveness programs. It's organized by state and has annotated and detailed listings about each program. To order a copy, write to the National College Scholarship Foundation, PO Box 8207, Gaithersburg, MD 20898-8207. The book is also offered through the Scholarship Resource Network, Inc., 44 Regatta View Drive, Saratoga Springs, NY 12866.

REPAYMENT ASSISTANCE PROGRAMS NOBODY TOLD YOU ABOUT

This next section contains some of the juiciest information in this book. Here's where I'll tell you about a number of loan repayment and assistance programs you've probably never heard of—but *should* have if the student loan system was working properly!

Your Employer to Your Financial Rescue

Worried about how you'll pay back those massive private loans or those huge federal loans? Well maybe *you* don't have to pay them back at all; maybe your *boss* will repay them. One of the best-kept secrets of the student loan universe is that many employers will happily pay off your college debts as part of an employment incentive contract. In other words, we're in a highly competitive, global economy and most employers want to hire good people. And when they get talented workers, they strive to keep them.

As a result, all across the country, a variety of employers, including hospitals and law enforcement organizations, colleges, law firms, state agencies, and federal entities are all offering cash-strapped employees a beauty of a perk in the form of student loan repayment assistance. Now don't expect to hear your employer shouting from the rooftop about this. Indeed, you may have to lobby to get it if no such program currently exists at your place of employment. But there's no reason that even those of you working in corporate America can't ask your boss about creating a student loan repayment program as a retention tool. Not only will it help you, but the cubicle mate next to you who's always complaining about his student loans will also be glad. With the exception of federal or government agencies that offer loan repayment programs, other employers can pay off your loans for you, including private loans for those of you with those debts.

The Feds Want You

One of the best programs I think you should know of is one that can help you if you're either looking for a job, currently working at a federal agency, or are willing to go to work in a government department or agency. It's called the Federal Student Loan Repayment Program, and it's remarkable in many aspects. Now, some of you might turn your nose up and frown at the prospect of working for the government. Before you do, however, let me point out the huge benefits of using your employment to get rid of your student loans.

Under the Federal Student Loan Repayment Program, the government allows any federal agency to repay your FFEL, direct, Perkins, or HEAL loans in order to attract or retain highly qualified workers in the federal government. Interestingly, each agency sets its own definition of highly qualified. Under the law, you don't even have to have a degree, certificate or some other diploma to qualify for this loan repayment assistance initiative. Therefore, even those of you who left college before you earned a degree—as one out of five students who take on college debts do drop out—can take advantage of this program.

The most comprehensive source of information about this program is maintained by the Office of Personnel Management (OPM). The place on their website where you can learn more about this program is *www.opm.gov.*

For now, though, just consider the possibilities under this tremendously powerful, but apparently underutilized, program that could help tons of college grads pay off their debts.

Let's say you're out of a job and you have been looking for work everywhere—except the federal government. Now is definitely the time to throw your hat into the ring to get a position with a federal agency. For an A to Z listing of all federal departments and agencies in America, go to the U.S. government's official Web portal at: *www.firstgov.gov/Agencies/Federal/All_Agencies/index.shtml.* I don't care what you studied in school: from architecture and art history to engineering, business, nursing, journalism, or even zoology, there's a job you can land at a federal agency where you could put your educational training, skills, and experience to use.

First of all, you have to know that all agencies exist within the three branches of the U.S. government: the executive branch, the judicial branch, and the legislative branch. Under the executive branch, all agencies are categorized by department, including:

- Executive Office of the President
- Department of Agriculture

- Department of Commerce
- Department of Defense
- Department of Education
- Department of Energy
- Department of Health and Human Services
- Department of Homeland Security
- Department of Housing and Urban Development
- Department of the Interior
- Department of Justice
- Department of Labor
- Department of State
- Department of Transportation
- Department of the Treasury
- Department of Veterans Affairs

Housed under each of these departments are scores of additional agencies where you can work. And remember: each one is in need of workers just like any other employer. That's why the Student Loan Repayment Program was launched as a recruitment tool, and as a device that federal agencies could use to retain top talent. After all, what better way to recruit or keep the best and brightest than to offer a slew of benefits and perks—including student loan repayments? So here's what you need to know about this powerful program that's just waiting to be used by smart—and deeply indebted—college graduates and others just like you.

By the way, if you never pictured yourself working for the government, or if you have a philosophical opposition to working for a federal agency, why not work for an independent agency or a quasi-federal agency? Independent agencies are those that exist outside of the departments of the executive branch of the U.S. government. These agencies were established through separate statutes passed by the Congress.

Here's a list of the agencies that fall under those areas:

- Advisory Council on Historic Preservation (ACHP)
- Agency for International Development (USAID)
- American Battle Monuments Commission (ABMC)
- AmeriCorps
- Appalachian Regional Commission (ARC)
- U.S. Arctic Research Commission (USARC)
- Central Intelligence Agency (CIA)
- Commission on Civil Rights (USCCR)
- Commission on Security and Cooperation in Europe (CSCE)
- Commodity Futures Trading Commission (CFTC)
- Consumer Product Safety Commission (CPSC)
- Corporation for National and Community Service (CNCS)
- Environmental Protection Agency (EPA)
- Export-Import Bank of the United States (ExIm)
- Federal Communications Commission (FCC)
- Federal Deposit Insurance Corporation (FDIC)
- Federal Election Commission (FEC)
- Federal Maritime Commission
- Federal Mine Safety and Health Review Commission (FMSHRC)
- Federal Reserve System (The Fed)
- Federal Retirement Thrift Investment Board
- Federal Trade Commission (FTC)
- General Services Administration (GSA)
- Institute of Museum and Library Services (IMLS)
- Inter-American Foundation (IAF)
- Learn and Serve America (LSA)
- National Aeronautics and Space Administration (NASA)
- National Archives and Records Administration (NARA)
- National Capital Planning Commission (NCPC)
- National Endowment for the Arts (NEA)
- National Endowment for the Humanities (NEH)
- National Ice Center (NIC)
- National Labor Relations Board (NLRB)

- National Railroad Passenger Corporation (Amtrak) (NRPC)
- National Science Foundation (NSF)
- National Transportation Research Center (NTRC)
- National Transportation Safety Board (NTSB)
- Nuclear Regulatory Commission (NRC)
- Office of Personnel Management (OPM)
- Peace Corps
- Pension Benefit Guaranty Corporation (PBGC)
- United States Postal Service (USPS)
- Postal Rate Commission (PRC)
- Securities and Exchange Commission (SEC)
- Office of Government Ethics (OGE)
- Selective Service System (SSS)
- Senior Corps
- Small Business Administration (SBA)
- Social Security Administration (SSA)
- Tennessee Valley Authority (TVA)

Quasi-federal agencies include the Legal Services Corporation (LSC) and the Smithsonian Institution. The LSC, established by Congress in 1974, is a private, nonprofit corporation designed to make sure all Americans have equal access to justice under the law, regardless of their income. The LSC offers legal help to Americans who otherwise couldn't afford it.

The Smithsonian Institution, as you probably know, is an educational and research institute and museum complex. It's funded by the U.S. government and by money from its own endowment, private contributions, and profits generated from its shops and its magazine. Although most Smithsonian facilities are located in Washington, DC, it also has 19 museums and 7 research centers elsewhere, including New York City, Virginia, and even Panama.

No matter whether you work for a federal agency that's under the executive branch, or an independent agency or a quasi-government organization, any federal employee is eligible to benefit from the

Student Loan Repayment Program—with the exception of so-called Schedule C appointees, because their jobs are often confidential and policy-making in nature.

Under this program, your loans aren't considered "forgiven," rather, your employer will make payments on your behalf directly to the holder of your student loan(s). Your employer can make up to $10,000 in student loan repayments per employee, per calendar year, up to a maximum of $60,000 per employee. If you're currently job-hunting, or are willing to switch jobs, all you have to do is land a job with a federal agency and advise your prospective employer that the way to get you to accept their employment offer is to sweeten their package by providing you with the Student Loan Repayment Program as a benefit.

If you already work for a government agency, half the battle is won. Now you just have to convince your boss to either create a Student Loan Repayment Program or let you take advantage of an existing program that may already be in place. Mercifully, the federal government hasn't made it difficult to do this. You can readily win your employer's support for this program by showing them how easy the program is to create and how little work is required on their behalf.

The hard part, if there's anything difficult at all in this process, will likely be in getting your employer to agree to shell out the extra dollars to your loan holder. But if you can make a case for why you deserve to have this benefit—adding, of course, that it will help retain you as an employee, in keeping with the purpose of this program—then you're well on your way to being financially liberated from as much as $60,000 worth of student loans.

By now, some of you are probably wondering, what's the catch? Well, yes, there is a catch. In fact, there are a few catches you need to know about. First, in exchange for your employer paying off your hefty student loans, you'll be required to sign an employment contract pledging to remain in the employment of the federal agency you're with for at least three years. If you quit, or if you get fired for cause or poor performance, you must reimburse your employer for all the benefits you received under the Student Loan Repayment Program. (If you jump ship for another federal job, however, there's no law that says you have to repay the money, unless that was specifically written in your agreement with your employer.)

Another catch is that you have to maintain an acceptable level of performance on the job to continue getting student loan repayments. It's up to you and your employer to work out the definition of what's acceptable. The entire Federal Student Loan Repayment program, by the way, is at the discretion of your boss. The law states that your employer can even create a program specifically made for you!

And the last catch: the payments made on your behalf will be counted, under IRS guidelines, as taxable income to you. If you have an especially supportive boss, or an employer who's really hot to get you to come work at their agency, you can negotiate to have your employer pay those taxes.

In case your boss or a prospective employer needs prodding, here's what you can tell them that they'd have to do:

- Create a plan, if none currently exists, that describes how the agency will implement the student loan repayment program;
- Pay the employer's share of Social Security and Medicare taxes on the loan repayment;
- Report the loan repayment and taxes withheld to the IRS and state or local jurisdictions if required;
- Keep records about the student loan repayment program;
- Give a brief, annual report to the Office of Personnel Management on the student loan repayment program. This written report must be supplied to OPM before January 1 of each year, for the previous fiscal year. The report must state such information as: how many employees received this benefit, the job classifications of the recipients, and the total cost to the federal government of providing the loan repayment.

OPM, in turn, uses the information supplied from each federal agency to compile its own annual report to Congress detailing the use of the student loan repayment program by federal agencies.

For more information on this program, visit the OPM website at *www.opm.gov*, or call OPM at 1-202-606-1800. To write to the agency, address your inquiries to:

> U.S. Office of Personnel Management
> 1900 E Street NW
> Washington, DC 20415

A final word on this: if you do receive financial assistance from your employer, when you file your federal taxes you'll report the student loan repayments made on your behalf as wages, on line 7 of Form 1040, or on line 1 of Form 1040EZ.

State Education Departments

You'd think that because education is such a high priority for so many Americans that your state and local officials would be screaming at their top of their lungs to help out students drowning in debt or to let them know about options that could help them better manage or pay off those debts. But nope. You have to take the initiative to get help, resources, and other information from these officials. And one good place to check is your state department of higher education. These agencies often have a wealth of information about student loan repayment programs, even if they don't spread the word about them or make that information as accessible as they should.

Health-Related Organizations

I've already told you about medical loan forgiveness programs. But if you work in the medical field in any capacity, you can also get a variety of health-related organizations to help you foot those student loan bills. For example, in California, both the Health Professions

Education Foundation and the California Medical Board offer loan repayment plans. Other state medical boards will help you pay off your student loans as well. In many cases, receiving aid won't even put you on the hit list with Uncle Sam.

According to IRS Publication 970, Tax Benefits for Education, "Loan repayment programs provide student loan repayment assistance to participants on the condition that those participants provide certain services, generally primary health services, in areas where shortages of these services exist. In tax years beginning before 2004, such amounts given to participants for the sole purpose of repaying their student loans were taxable to the recipients."

Beginning in 2004, student loan repayment assistance you receive under the following programs is tax free:

- National Health Service Corps (NHSC) Loan Repayment Program
- State programs eligible for funds under the Public Health Service Act

The overall lesson is here is to be diligent in your search for loan repayment programs that can come to your aid. Look into the wealth of resources I've steered you to in this chapter, and take it one step further by thinking creatively about additional individuals, organizations, or institutions that might be willing to pay off your student loans. The key is to find a well-heeled source that is willing to fork over the money either because it's in their own best interest to do so (as in the case of an employer), or because it would simply be serving the public's best interest.

■ Part Three

Build Great Credit

10

WIPE OUT CREDIT CARD DEBT

Free Yourself from America's #1 Financial Plague

While student loans are a huge financial burden, it certainly isn't the only form of debt that most college grads carry. According to the College Board, the average student graduates from college with more than $2,700 in credit card bills. That's just the average, of course. Many students have lots more debt than that; some have none. But if you've been battling the credit card blues, take heart. You can whip that seemingly unbeatable monster called credit card debt. You just have to know the best strategies to do it—and be willing to implement a proper plan of action.

ATTACK YOUR AREA OF PAIN: HOW TO BEAT THE MINIMUM PAYMENT TRAP AND PAY OFF DEBTS FAST

I'm frequently asked by people which debts they should pay off first. In many cases, the underlying assumption is that people should pay off their cards with high interest rates first. In my previous book,

Zero Debt: The Ultimate Guide to Financial Freedom, I talk about this assumption and about the way in which I think that most people should pay off debts.

Personally, I do not agree with 99 percent of the experts out there who say you should pay off the high-interest debt first. My reasoning is simple: that strategy didn't work for me when I had $100,000 in credit card debt. And frankly, I haven't seen it work for thousands of others of people who are struggling with credit card bills despite their best efforts to tame the credit card beast month after month, or year after year. I believe you must attack your area of pain first to get the psychic and economic rewards of paying off your debts, and to keep yourself motivated.

I managed to pay off my debts in three years—without paying off the cards with the highest interest rate first. Some of you may wonder how that is possible, or even why I would not pay off high-rate debt first. Well, in my case, the problem wasn't really that I had high interest rates at all. In fact, even though I had a massive amount of credit card debt, I never missed a single payment. That kept me in good graces with my creditors, and allowed me to maintain relatively low interest rates. When I called up creditors to negotiate, I had leverage.

If a card had a moderate interest rate, with one simple phone call I was usually able to get it knocked down. At one point, all of my credit cards had interest rates below 6.9 percent. I had some at 4.9 percent and several, in fact, that were at 0 percent. The point I'm getting to is that for many consumers, the interest rate on their debt is not the true problem. The real culprit may be something else.

When you start considering which debts to pay off first, you have to determine the true source of your angst, so you can attack it. In general, there are three big problem areas for people battling credit card debt.

1. For some people, the interest rate is the chief problem. If the interest rates on your credit cards are sky—high- and I'm talking 20 to 30 percent—then I can see why you

might be going crazy about how much extra money you're forking over to the credit card companies. You might get discouraged paying those bills month after month and barely seeing your balance budge. That can be downright depressing. If it's the interest rate that's killing you, by all means attack that high-interest rate debt first.

2. For others, it's the high balance. What if your interest rates are in line with the national average—say 15 percent or so, or you have relatively low interest rates? Clearly, simply focusing on the cards with the highest interest rate won't do much for you. The truth of the matter is that some are driven bananas by the fact that they have large dollar balances on their accounts. They couldn't care less what the interest rate is on their cards. The interest rates on your cards may be high, low, or in-between, but if you're carrying so much debt that you're feeling squeezed, it could be that your area of pain is the amount of debt you have.

   Nobody likes that anxiety-provoking feeling that comes along with being maxed out. And who wants to worry, when you're out at a restaurant or using your card in a store, whether your credit card will be accepted or declined because you're right at or near your limit? How embarrassing! I know because it happened to me when I maxed out my credit cards. If this sounds like your situation, what may really be driving you crazy is having cards without high dollar balances.

3. Maybe you have too many accounts. Others among you may be driven into a frenzy by having multiple accounts. In fact, you may have so many credit cards that you find it overwhelming. Do you have difficultly juggling your payments each month because you have so many cards that you actually forget about some that are due? Or do you have so many credit cards that you have trouble simply keeping track of all the bills and organizing those monthly

statements that never stop coming? When you get over-
whelmed by the sheer number of cards, and find yourself
unable to properly manage those accounts, you may find
yourself forgetting payments, accidentally misplacing
statements, and making other mistakes that cause you to
get hit with late fees or dinged with other miscellaneous
charges from your credit card companies.

For the last two scenarios—if you have cards with high dollar balances, or if it's the stress of juggling multiple accounts that is bugging
you—then attack those areas of your pain first.

For those of you troubled by high dollar balances, start devoting
a bigger portion of your credit card repayments to those accounts
that are maxed out, or close to being maxed out. You'll gradually
start to see those balances decline, and your stress level will simulta-
neously decline.

If you're stressed out over carrying what seems like an entire
deck of credit cards in your wallet, begin by paying off the credit card
with the lowest dollar balance first. This way, you'll knock out a small
account, eliminate one card from your list, and you can apply the
money that you were putting on that card to the next card. In this
method, you'll automatically decrease the number of cards you're
carrying, as well as more quickly shrink your overall debt load.

The reason the attack to your area of pain method works better
than the blanket pay off high-rate debt first advice is that you're more
likely to stick with something that's giving you results—emotionally
and financially. Part of the reason people can't or don't pay off debts
using the high interest rate payment first method is because it doesn't
always take into account what's troubling them.

And for people to stay motivated and stick to a game plan—in
this case, a long-term credit card repayment plan—they have to feel
like they're getting the benefits of doing so. It's depressing to just pay
bills month after month and not feel like you're making any head-
way on those debts. But if you knock out a debt after two or three

months—as you can in the case of paying off cards with low dollars balances first—imagine the satisfaction you'll get at seeing those liabilities dwindle. That's what produces long-term results and gets you to stick with your repayment plan.

TIPS FOR NEGOTIATIONS WITH CREDITORS

Negotiating with your creditors is one of the hands-down best ways to manage and ultimately reduce your credit card bills. So many people neglect this option, however, because they are either afraid to do it, or unaware that they can negotiate to get some relief from those ever-growing credit card balances.

But there comes a time in most people's lives when they have slipped up with their credit in some way or another. Many of us have had excessive amounts of credit card debt. Some people have fallen behind on auto payments. Some individuals even skipped mortgage payments, and faced foreclosure, bankruptcy, or other financial calamities. No matter what your current or past predicament, there are a lot of things that you can do to get out of problem situations with your creditors.

You can negotiate to lower your interest rates or to have certain negative marks removed from your credit report. You can also get the total amount of debt you owe knocked down considerably by negotiating. So one of the first things I always tell people who are facing a financial problem is that you can dig yourself out of this hole if you face the situation head on. You do not have to feel that the world is going to cave in on you just because you owe somebody or just because you slipped up with credit and had problems in the past. For many of you, I hope that just knowing that there is a solution and a way out of this mess will give you some consolation and optimism for the future.

While many of the negotiating strategies I will suggest in this chapter pertain primarily to those of you with credit card debt, in certain cases, these very same strategies can also be used on any kind of debt that you might owe, whether it is a mortgage debt, an auto loan, medical bills, or other obligations.

Negotiate with the Right Person

Whenever you're trying to negotiate with a creditor, if the person on the phone says no, feel free to elevate your request a level. Ask to speak to a supervisor who may be empowered to wheel and deal, and who may have more authority to cut you a deal. One main strategy is to know whom to talk to and at what point a person with more authority needs to join the conversation.

For some requests, frankly, you do not need to go to a supervisor. People often ask me whether they should immediately ask for a supervisor when calling up to negotiate with a creditor. My answer is no, it's not always necessary or prudent. In some instances, the customer service rep on the phone can say yes to your request. Sometimes, you'll also need to put your request in writing. Clearly, if you come up against a customer service representative who is very difficult, belligerent, or very inflexible and will not waive a bit, then by all means take the time to speak to a supervisor. Always ask politely for their boss, because if you don't, you may be "accidentally" disconnected while they put you on hold for the supervisor.

Get Late Fees Removed Easily

Even when you're dealing with the line workers, the customer service reps, 99 percent or more have the power to do things like eliminate a late fee on your credit card account at least one time every 12 months. But they are not going to volunteer do this. They won't call you up and offer it to you.

So if you don't know to initiate that conversation and ask for a late fee to be eliminated or ask for an over-the-limit charge to be waived, it won't happen. I personally have done this several times where, either I have been traveling or busy or just simply forgot. And for whatever reason, a bill went unpaid. If I ever saw a late fee on my credit card statement, even if the check got mailed and processed in the credit card company's system the day after the due date, I would immediate call up the company and ask them to waive the late fee. In the three or four times I've done this, the customer service rep took a look at my track record, agree that it was an aberration, and immediately removed the late fee.

You can call them up and do the same thing. You'll find that the operator will say something like "OK, I can waive that fee for you as a courtesy," or "I can remove this charge this time." Obviously, this is not something you should abuse. You can't try to take advantage of the system by paying your Visa, MasterCard, or other credit card bills late every other month, and then expecting to call up your creditors and constantly get late fees removed. That won't work.

When you call, you don't even need to give a reason. (You can, if you have a good one.) But it's probably best to simply say, "I noticed a late charge on my most recent statement. I'm sorry the bill was inadvertently paid late. I'll make sure it doesn't happen again. In the meantime, I'm calling to request that you waive the late fee in this instance."

Having a good payment track record will undoubtedly work in your favor when you make this kind of request, but even for those of you with occasional lapses, you can get late payments removed at least once a year.

Handle Simple Matters via Telephone

While certain deals you strike with bill collectors should be cemented in writing, don't make the mistake of thinking every correspondence you have with your credit card company needs to be put down in black and white. No sense in sitting down at a computer, mulling over a situation, and spending 30 minutes typing a letter over something minor. Just pick up the phone and call the toll-free number

Pick Up the Phone for These Issues

- An erroneous balance amount
- An incorrect interest rate
- A charge that you did not make or authorize
- Late charges
- Over-the-limit penalties
- Miscellaneous fees for unwanted products or services, such as credit insurance protection
- An unwarranted or unexpected change in the terms of your agreement, like a lowering of your credit limit

listed on your credit card statement, and explain the situation. If it is clearly something that is an error on their part, nine times out of ten, you can get it readily resolved over the telephone.

The challenge for you is to follow up after they say, "Yes, we will waive that fee," or "You're right, we were not supposed to charge you that annual fee." You'll have to check your statement for the next month or two to make sure the fees have been removed, credited to your account, or that whatever error you spotted has been fixed.

Confirm Serious Negotiations in Writing

For bigger disputes, as may be the case if you signed up for a card at a specific rate and they suddenly say it's another rate, by all means do send a letter to the creditor. If you are attempting to negotiate a settlement of some type, I would definitely say start with the phone call and see whether or not you have a receptive customer service representative or a very responsive supervisor. After you settle on some terms and create an agreement, solidify your agreement in writing.

If you're dealing with olds debts, especially, and you're trying to clean up your credit, you may have to do a bit of a dance with your creditors. They know that a lot of times when people pop up offering to settle accounts that are more than one, two, or three years old, those

Sample Settlement Letter to a Credit Card Company

Dear Stephanie Jones, customer service representative for XYZ,

Per our conversation of XYZ date, you have agreed to accept $600 as payment in full for account #XYZ, which previously was noted as having an account balance of $1,000. According to the terms of our agreement, I will pay you the $600 in full and in exchange, you will remove all negative references on this account to TransUnion, Equifax, and Experian. Please sign this letter and date it, and send it back to me and a payment will be forthcoming immediately upon me receiving your signed acknowledgment of this agreement.

The letter can be as simple as that. You can send the letter via fax, e-mail, or snail mail. But I recommend putting it in the mail, and sending your letter certified mail, return receipt requested. Again, I cannot tell you the number of people I have talked to who said, "I did send the bill, but they claimed they did not even get the payment." Well, your proof is asking the U.S. Post Office for a record, and that documentation can be obtained in the form of a proof of delivery.

individuals usually have a good reason for wanting to all of a sudden get this matter cleared up and removed from their credit reports.

But what's in it for the creditors is that they are getting some cash upfront and they have already written off your debt. They have already taken a tax deduction on that and basically reported your debt as a loss on their books to the IRS. So the fact that they are getting some money now as supposed to having gotten no money over the last couple of years makes them somewhat flexible and willing to negotiate. On your side of the equation what is in it for you is that in order for you to give up that money—and you certainly want to make a lump sum payment or a few installment payments—you want to see that late notation or any negative marks deleted from your credit file.

I cannot tell you how many people write to tell me that they negotiated something over the telephone and then they thought they had an understanding, or they sent in money to settle an account or to bring current an account that was past due, only to find out that their account still was being reported to the Big Three credit bureaus—TransUnion, Equifax, and Experian—as being delinquent or past due.

Sometimes, it seems that the creditor they negotiated with simply made them a deal and did not hold up their end of the bargain at all. The way that you could get around that is after your make a phone deal where you work out something or negotiate a settlement, put everything in writing. In many cases, it will be more expedient and more advantageous to you if you create the letter of agreement. Basically, all you have to do is summarize the discussion.

Request a Lower Interest Rate and More

What are some other things that you should do when you are in the process of negotiating?

- You can ask for your interest rates to be lowered, especially since the average credit card has about a 15 percent interest rate right now.
- You can ask your credit card company to stop late fees, or to eliminate over-the-limit charges.
- You can ask them to upgrade your account to current status.
- You can certainly ask them to remove negative marks from your credit file.
- You can ask them to accept the partial payments in lieu of the total amount due.
- Get creative, think about what your particular needs are and do not be afraid to ask for what you need.

A lower interest rate should be something everyone tries to secure. It could be yours for the asking, but you have to get comfortable with getting on the phone and asking for it because they are certainly not going to do that for you. Part of the reason you have leverage to negotiate with your creditors is that credit card companies send out between four and five billion credit card offers each year, according to the Consumer Federation of America. That means you have leverage with credit card companies because they know that there's stiff competition out there. Lots of other credit card companies can and will vie for your business, so your credit card company doesn't want to lose you as a client and miss out on that stream of income you represent in the form of interest payments.

CALL YOUR CREDITORS WHEN YOU FACE THE "DREADED Ds"

One of the biggest disservices that we do to ourselves as consumers is when we hide from the credit card company or others we owe. Credit card companies shouldn't have to hunt you down. In fact, there are five times when you should be the one to initiate a phone call with your creditors. These five instances revolve around what I call the Dreaded Ds, referring to the time in your life when you might suffer a:

- Downsizing
- Divorce
- Death in the family of the main breadwinner
- Disease
- Disability

If any one of those five things happens to you or somebody close in your family, it can totally throw your finances out of whack and it could definitely make you wind up in debt. So if get a pink slip, you find yourself in the throws of a divorce, or you wind up sick and disabled, don't be like the ostrich that sticks its head in the sand. Ignoring the problem won't make the bills go away. Pick up the phone, call your credit card company immediately, and explain your situation.

Request Mortgage Payment Relief If Necessary

If you have a mortgage, pick up the phone and call your lender as well. You might not necessarily need to ask for forbearance or deferment or any kind, but you should definitely let them know about your changed circumstances. Say something like, "At this time, this is my situation. I've just received a notice from my company that I am going to be downsized and I am going to be terminated as of X date in the future," or "I have just been terminated effective immediately, is there anything that your company offers for people who are in my situation?"

You may be surprised to learn that lenders of every kind have many different programs and offering to help clients with financial problems. For example, if that creditor happens to be a mortgage company, do you realize that they have "workout" programs, as they call it? I used to be a *Wall Street Journal* reporter for CNBC. And when I was on air at CNBC, I will never forget doing a TV report on how to prevent foreclosure.

The gist of what I learned is that most banks, and certainly the large mortgage lenders, have entire departments devoted to helping down-on-their luck customers. Countrywide, for example, has a full-fledged division called the workout department that is designed to do nothing but aid consumers who have experienced financial difficulties. Their goal is to help you to get back on track. When they send letters or call, it's not that they are trying to harass you. They're trying to find out what is the situation, what is the problem, how long will it take for you to recover, and what can be done in the meantime to help you.

Restructure the Terms of Your Payment

Some credit card companies and banks will say, OK, if you can't pay for two or three months right now, we'll let you forgo those payments in the short term and will add those payments to the back end of your loan in order to help you come current and get back on track. Of course, these businesses aren't doing this out of the kindness of their hearts. They do not want you to go into foreclosure. They do not want you to be delinquent in your mortgage payments. They do not want you to wind up in bankruptcy court, because that is not financially advantageous for them because they risk getting nothing. That's why they've designed programs to assist you to through tough times.

By tacking on payments on the back end, or deferring payments, interest still accrues in many cases, but at least your credit card company or mortgage lender allows you to preserve your credit rating and not get dinged with 30-, 60- or 90-day past due payments. Those are credit killers in the long run and can hurt you for many years to come.

Revise Your Credit Card Due Dates

You can also ask your creditors to change the due dates on your accounts. Why would want to do this? Well, this is a negotiation that really helps you to deal with cash flow issues. Some of you may have all your bills coming due around the first or the tenth of the month. Well, you can call up your creditors and say, "Can you switch the due date on my account from the first of the month to the 20th?" The point of you doing this is that you're going to be able to spread out your payments to meet your own unique cash flow situation, so all your bills won't come due around the same exact time.

Begin Settlement Negotiations with a Lowball Offer

If you have past due accounts that are significantly overdue, and you're now ready to settle up and pay off those accounts, don't hesitate to start with a low offer. Call up your creditor and start negotiating by offering no more than 50 cents on the dollar—particularly if it's your first round of negotiation, and especially if it is an old account.

In many cases, the creditor will have already written off the account, meaning they've already taken a tax loss from on the account. And because they have not seen or heard from you in whatever amount of time, it's a bonus (in their eyes) for them to get a call from you. So for them to get some money is better than getting no money at all. Also, if you are serious about rebuilding your credit, you only want to pay those institutions, lenders, and organizations that agree to delete all negative information from your credit report in exchange for your payments. That should be high on your priority list.

If they can't agree to that condition, I would suggest moving on to the next account and negotiating with the next creditor. The strategy is to concentrate on paying off those old debts that you can get removed from your credit report entirely.

UNDERSTAND CREDIT REPORTING LAWS

Negative information can legally stay on your credit report for seven years, and a bankruptcy can stay in your credit report for ten years. After seven years, you are entitled to have that negative information removed. But understand this little-known fact: your credit information can be reported seven years from the date of last activity.

This is something that trips up most consumers. It's not seven years ago since you last had the bill. It's seven years since the account had any activity on it. So let's say a creditor of bill collector called up two years ago and reminded you about a debt. And just to get them off your back, you went ahead and sent in a payment, even a small one of just say, $50. Do you realize that you've just restarted the clock, and so now it is another seven years?

Now any negative information, such as a nonpayment for 30 days or more, will be on your credit report for another seven years from the time you made that payment, unless you make other settlement arrangements with your credit. Let me say that I'm not suggesting that you shirk your financial duties. I believe in paying your bills. I also believe that you should take responsibility for your obligations because nobody put a gun to your head and forced you to run up credit card bills.

But we all know that people get into debt for a whole host of reasons, many of which have absolutely nothing to do with lavish spending. I'm talking about individuals, couples, and families that get deep in debt because of job loss, death of a main breadwinner, medical bills, and other crises outside their control.

CONSIDER BANKRUPTCY AS A LAST-DITCH OPTION

Fortunately, if you are financially unable to pay your bills, this country has a system designed to help you to eliminate those debts. It is called *bankruptcy*. And although bankruptcy laws have been reformed in late 2005—and I only recommend bankruptcy as a last resort—you should nevertheless know about your options.

The fact of the matter is that a lot of people are technically bankrupt yet struggling day to day to keep their heads above water. If you are contemplating bankruptcy because you're being hounded by creditors, and your cash flow situation is dire, make a point to get on the phone to negotiate and first try to settle your debts. If you have bills that are very old, seven years old or approaching that time, those debts would be very, very low on my list of priorities to repay, if at all.

GET A FRESH START WITH CREDITORS WITHOUT BANKRUPTCY

Let's turn now to a discussion of how you can get a fresh start with your creditors—and I'm not talking about filing for bankruptcy protection. Have you ever heard of something called re-aging for your credit card accounts? When you have your accounts re-aged, negative information about your past-due accounts—such as notations about 30- or 60-day late payments—gets wiped clean from your credit file.

Re-aging also has other benefits too. Yet, most people have never heard of this process, despite the fact that it could help millions of consumers who are struggling with credit and debt issues. If only they knew what to do, where to start, and how they could go about getting their accounts re-aged. I'm going to share that information with you now. But first let me take a moment to talk to you about why it is that the "age" of your accounts matters at all.

The Average Age of Your Accounts

I've previously explained the importance of your FICO score. But as a recap, FICO stands for Fair Isaac Corporation, which is the business that compiles credit scores for millions of people nationwide. Your FICO credit score is based on five different things, the most important of which is your payment history—in other words, your track record of paying your bills on time. That accounts for 35 percent of your FICO score. But another thing that goes into computing your FICO score is the length of your credit history, which is sometimes known as the average age of your accounts.

Generally speaking, people with a longer credit history have better FICO credit scores. Therefore, if you just opened your very first credit card or just got your first mortgage six months ago, the average age of that account is six months. But if you've had a mortgage for 10 years, that has a 120-month history, so the average age of that account is far greater. Over time, the longer you hold on to credit cards, or the longer that you pay your mortgages, the longer that you pay those auto loans and so on, the higher the average age of your accounts. And increasing the average age of your accounts is generally a positive thing for your FICO credit score.

Unfortunately, some people shoot themselves in the foot when it comes to messing with the age of their accounts—namely by closing out old accounts. When someone closes a credit card they've had

Have You Made This Common Credit Mistake?

When you finally pay off a credit card or transfer balances from one credit card to another, in most cases it's best *not* to close out your old account. Nevertheless, a common misconception among consumers is that getting rid of credit cards will improve your FICO credit score. But it usually won't. In fact, closing old accounts could backfire, causing your FICO credit score to drop because you've decreased the average age of your accounts and you've increased the percentage of credit used versus the amount of credit you have available, according to experts at Fair Isaac, the credit scoring company.

for a really long time, they cut off that past payment history, and decrease the average age of their accounts, most often resulting in a lower credit score.

Re-Age an Overdue Credit Card to Improve Your Credit

But what if you've had an overdue credit card or an account that has gone past due and you want that negative information wiped off of your credit records? Well, the process of re-aging is how you get a "do over" in the credit card world. Re-aging is the way in which you get a second chance with your creditors if you've slipped up and let an account go past due.

With re-aging, almost like magic, your past-due account gets "re-aged" and presto, all of a sudden that overdue due account gets zapped back to current status. It gets taken out of late payment status in terms of being shown as 30, 60, or 90 days past due, and you get a fresh start on your account. Basically, re-aging provides you with a fresh slate on your credit card history. If you had a credit card for five years, it had a 60-month history. But with re-aging, you've started the clock again as if the card was brand new, with a one month history.

Re-aging doesn't absolve you of your responsibility to pay your debts. But the late fees stop, and your credit file improves because the negative information is erased. And if you can get a company to re-age your account, then those late fees that they might have been charging you or any extra interest you've been paying on those bills can also be eliminated.

How to Qualify to Get Your Account Re-Aged

There are federal rules that dictate who can get their accounts re-aged, and under what circumstances. The rules and regulations concerning re-aging are established by an organization called the Federal Financial Institutions Examination Council. In the year 2000, that entity established rules for re-aging. It said that in order to be considered for re-aging, the following criteria must be met:

- As a borrower, you have to demonstrate that you have the willingness and ability to pay the debt, whatever it might be.
- If it is a credit card account, it has to be at least nine months old. In other words, if you got this card three or four months ago and you slipped up and are already 30, 60, or 90 days past due, this account is not going to be eligible to be re-aged.
- You should also make three consecutive payments at least of the minimum monthly payments that are due. Therefore, you can't just pay some nominal amount or an arbitrary figure based on what you can afford on any given month. You must make the minimum monthly payments required for three consecutive months.
- There is a limit on the number of times you can have an account re-aged. Creditors can only do this once every 12 months and they can only do it twice in a five-year period.
- The accounts being re-aged must be what the credit industry terms as open ended accounts.

Re-aging is an especially beneficial thing if your account was previously very overdue, say a year or more, and you've started making repayments. Remember: by getting an account re-aged, you are sort of setting the clock back in terms of starting over the life of that account, because now it is going to be reflected on your credit report from this point on, as if it is a new account. So that is one of the caveats to doing this procedure.

If you only have two accounts for instance, and one of them gets re-aged you don't want to lower the overall average age of your accounts to such a level that it actually winds up hurting your FICO score. With these basic rules in mind, you may want to call up your creditor and request that they re-age your account.

Sometimes various credit card companies and other financial institutions will only do it if you enter a debt management plan, start some kind of credit counseling program, or if you start some kind of debt workout program. In those instances, they will readily agree to re-age that past due account and bring it up to current status. Once again, you first have to meet those requirements—showing that you actually have the money and the ability to pay the debt; and making those minimum monthly payments three months in a row, and so forth. But even without entering some kind of debt management or credit counseling program, you can get your account re-aged.

Based on the information in this chapter, I hope you feel empowered to negotiate with your creditors, and that you've decided on a credit card repayment strategy that will attack your area of pain. Having paid off a mountain of credit card debt myself, I know that becoming debt-free is feasible for most people.

While you're paying off your student loans and credit cards debts, you'll also want to do everything in your power to develop and maintain an outstanding credit rating. The next chapter will give you some pointers on how to do just that. By building a stellar credit profile, you'll strengthen your overall financial status, wind up with more dollars in your bank account, and you'll enjoy all the personal, professional, and economic benefits that come with having great credit.

11

ESTABLISH GREAT CREDIT
The Three-Digit Number That's More Important Than Your GPA

I've told you already about how absolutely vital it is that you maintain great credit. Your credit score is used by lenders, employers, and others as an indication of your character and how financially responsible you are. So it pays to know what you can do to establish great credit or improve your credit tremendously if you have blemishes in your credit file. Anything you can do to bolster your credit standing will save you lots of money, and will help you become financially free as well. But it's smart to start by knowing about some basic things that are impacting your credit score—as well as what isn't.

SECRETS TO BOOSTING YOUR FICO CREDIT SCORE

Let's talk about how you can boost that almighty FICO credit score. Your FICO score is a critical three-digit number that tells people a heck of a lot about you from a financial perspective. Your FICO score ranges from 300 to 850; the higher your score, the better a lending risk you're deemed. In my life, I have only known one person who had a perfect 850 FICO credit score. This is something that is so rare that even most loan officers and bankers say they're never seen a perfect 850 FICO score.

While you don't need to achieve absolute perfection, I do think that having a FICO score in the range of "perfect credit" is a good and worthwhile goal. When I say *perfect credit*, I'm really referring to a FICO score in the 760 to 850 point range. With a score in this upper tier, you are golden in the financial universe. Lenders will fall all themselves trying to compete for your business.

You'll get practically all the credit you could ever want, and at the best rates possible. I'm talking the most attractive rates and terms on everything from mortgages, to auto loans, to small business loans, to personal loans, home equity, credit cards, you name it. If you have a 760 to 850 FICO score, you are a favored customer in the eyes of all lenders. So what does it takes to boost your FICO credit score and get in into the top range? Certainly, one of the things to do is to fix any mistakes that might be on your credit report as I described earlier. Beyond that, though, the best way to raise that FICO score is to take some advice straight from the horse's mouth.

The folks at Fair Isaac say that five different elements are considered when they calculate your FICO score. Before I tell you what those five criteria are, you should know that the whole process of credit scoring used to be completely shrouded in mystery. People had no clue about what it took to increase their credit score or why it was, in fact, that their FICO score was a 580, 680, or 780.

Several years ago, however, Fair Isaac disclosed to the public the five different components that go into computing your FICO score. They are as follows:

1. About 35 percent, the biggest part of your FICO score, is based on your payment history. In other words, how well you have paid your bills. This demonstrates your track record of honoring your obligations in a timely, agreed-upon fashion.

2. About 30 percent of your FICO score is based on the amount of debt that you have outstanding. How much you owe others shows whether or not you can manage credit and debt well, or whether you overdose on debt.

3. About 15 percent of your FICO score it is based on the length of your credit history. Generally, the longer your credit history, the more positively that weighs on your FICO credit score.

4. About 10 percent of your FICO score is based on new credit that you establish. This is where inquiries and new applications for credit come into play.

5. And then the final 10 percent of your FICO score has to do with the type of credit that you have in use. The mix of credit that you are currently using as a consumer is gauged by the variety of accounts you have, such as mortgage, major credit cards, retail cards, and so forth.

So, what does all this tell you in terms of being able to boost your FICO score? Well, it tells you a lot. First, the most heavily weighted areas pertain to your debts outstanding (30 percent), and to your ability to simply make your payments on time (35 percent). I've interviewed Fair Isaac representatives and they told me very clearly that the single best thing you can do to boost your FICO credit score is to just pay your bills on time. It is as simple as that. Other strategies can obviously help. But over time, let's say for six months or a year, if you literally did nothing else (that is, you didn't apply for any new credit, you didn't close any accounts, etc.) your credit score would increase over time merely by you making timely monthly payments.

Don't Skip Bills

You can't afford to skip any bills—and I mean *any* bills, ever. Not the mortgage, not your credit card payments, not car payments. It's not just delinquent student loans or overdue medical bills that can ruin your credit. You probably will be shocked to know that the slight-est infraction may get reported in your credit file—anything from a late payment on your cell phone bill to a skipped payment to your utility company. You might even fall out of your chair to know that some libraries are even reporting people who have turned in the li-brary books late! Yes, even a late library book can show up on your credit report.

I've heard, too, of some cities and municipalities taking a hard line on unpaid parking tickets. In various jurisdictions, those unpaid tickets are also being reported on people's credit report, thereby low-ering their FICO credit score. The lesson here, therefore, is to do everything within your power to always, always pay your bills on time, no matter how small or insignificant they may seem. Otherwise, all the hard work you put in on paying those big bills on time—like your mortgage or student loans—could be undone when a small bill winds up damaging your credit report.

None of this is to suggest that you never have to prioritize your bills. Don't get me wrong: in a dire cash crunch, clearly the mortgage takes the precedent over the cell phone bill. Nevertheless, your goal should be to pay every single bill on time, every single month, with-out fail. That is the best thing you can do to raise your FICO score.

Pay Down Your Debt

What about the amounts owed on your credit card accounts and other bills? The experts at Fair Isaac tell me that shifting debt around is not going to boost your credit score by and large. You have to pay that debt down. Some people think, "Because I am maxed out on this credit card and I got another credit card offer in the mail, I'll just shift my balance over to the new card, and get some breathing room." While it's true that the balance on that first card will be lowered or eliminated altogether, it's also true that the total amount of debt you owe will remain the same.

Fair Isaac officials haven't specifically said what is the ideal amount of debt for a person to keep in order to maximize your FICO score. However, it's widely believed that you should never use more than 50 percent of the credit that is available to you. My own best estimation, based on my research and my knowledge of the overall Fair Isaac credit scoring model, is that you'll be scored more favorable if you use 25 percent or less of the credit that is available to you. Therefore, if you have three credit cards, and each of them has a $10,000 credit line available to you, ideally, you should not carry a balance of more than $2,500 on any of those cards. Many people, though, find themselves far above that range.

Maybe you're one of them. Perhaps you're maxed out on our credit cards, or you've already used 50, 60, 70 percent or more of your available credit. This percentage of credit you've used versus the amount of credit you have available is called your credit utilization rate. Pay your debts instead of shifting debt around, and try your best to keep your credit utilization rate as low as possible in order to achieve the highest possible FICO credit score.

Build a Credit History

The length of your credit history also plays a role in your FICO credit score. Generally, the longer you have been in the credit game, the longer you have had a credit history, the more likely it is that you will have a higher FICO score.

New credit refers to inquiries, or those new credit applications that you seek out from lenders. To improve your FICO score, don't apply for too many credit offers or seek out credit unnecessarily. You have to demonstrate that you can manage the credit you have well. Or, if you do amass new credit, it's better to accumulate that additional credit slowly, building it up over time. Don't make the mistake that a lot of people make by going on a credit-application spree, opening all kinds of credit cards and taking on new loans without so much as a second thought.

Remember: the types of credit that you have in use plays a role in your FICO score—it's 10 percent of it. You should also know that certain types of debt are deemed more favorably, helping to boost your FICO credit score. On the other hand, certain kinds of loans—for example, department store credit cards or consumer finance loans—are deemed poorly from a credit scoring standpoint. Those tend to lower your FICO credit score.

So the prudent thing to do is to focus on managing your existing credit, not applying for new credit unless you absolutely need it, and then only obtaining credit from the right types of sources—those that will bolster your credit score, and not hurt it.

Don't Transfer Balances the Wrong Way!

What about transferring high-interest rate credit card balances? Will that improve your credit score? Usually it will not—although it can save you money in finance charges in the long run. If you ever want to transfer balances from one credit card to another, keep these five tips in mind.

1. Do not close out those old accounts! This is the most important rule. Think back to the five different components that go into calculating your FICO credit score. The experts at Fair Isaac say that it is a misconception among consumers that closing an old account will raise their credit score. The truth is that it won't. What's worse is that in many cases, closing out an old account can actually have the opposite intended effect, and can lower your FICO credit score.

    The reason is that, even if you transfer a balance to a card under a 0 percent balance transfer deal, if you close out your original account, you will be purging your credit history and decreasing the average age of your accounts. That account you close may have been one with considerable longevity. You might have had it for three, five, seven years, or more. But now, just because you transferred a balanced to a lower rate card (one with a low rate for a temporary period, I might add), you've made the classic mistake of wiping out your seven-year track record of paying another credit card on time.

2. Don't reopen an account after you've closed it. Some people, upon learning of the mistake they've made in closing out an old account, will ask me whether they should reopen the account. My answer is no, do not try to reopen it because, again, you could be shooting yourself in the foot, and hurting your credit score. Getting the account reopened means you'll have another inquiry on your credit file, and you'll have to apply for a new line of credit. It's better to simply learn the lesson and not make this mistake again in the future.

3. Don't ruin your credit utilization rate. Another classic mistake people make in initiating balance transfers is that they ruin their credit utilization rate, once again hurting their FICO credit score. Here's an example of how this is commonly done.

    Let's say you have two credit cards—a MasterCard and a Visa, and each has a $10,000 credit limit. Let's further assume that you've charged $5,000 on each card. Therefore, your credit utilization rate is 50 percent. In other words, you've charged a total of $10,000 and you have a total of $20,000 in credit at your disposal.

    Now let's say you get a wonderful credit card offer in the mail from Discover. Since your Visa and MasterCard carry interest rates of 14.9 percent and 17.9 percent, respectively, and Discover is offering you a 4.9 percent balance transfer deal, you jump at this offer in a bid to save money on finance charges.

    The problem arises, however, when Discover tells you that you've been approved for a $10,000 credit line. But the company is willing to let you transfer balances from both your Visa and MasterCard up to the full $10,000 limit on your Discover-even with no over-the-limit charges—in order to help you save money.

Naturally, you take Discover up on its offer, and those $10,000 worth of charges that were sitting on your Visa and MasterCard bill get transferred over to your new Discover card. Moreover, you close out your old accounts with Visa and MasterCard. You're thinking, "Ha! I've beat the system. I'll be saving lots of money as a result of these smart balance transfers!" But take a look at what happens next in the credit scoring world.

Previously, you had a 50 percent credit utilization rate, because you'd charged $10,000 and had $20,000 worth of credit available to you. Now, your credit utilization rate jumps to 100 percent. You haven't charged a single additional dime. But because you have $10,000 worth of debt on a single card with a $10,000 limit, statistically, the FICO credit scoring model looks at you as a person who is maxed out on your cards. Not so smart, is it?

Adding further insult to injury, you've also lowered your credit score by closing those old accounts and decreasing the average age of your accounts. All you have now is a brand-spanking new Discover card with a one-month history; previously you had a MasterCard with a five year, or 60-month history, and a Visa with a seven year, or 84-month history.

Do you see how people can easily get tripped up if they make some common mistakes with credit and debt? One potential solution is to request a higher limit from Discover. A $20,000 limit would preserve your 50 percent credit utilization rate if you closed out the Visa and MasterCard accounts. Of course, a better strategy is to also refrain from closing out those old accounts.

4. Know the fees and terms imposed by credit card compa-

nies. Many banks will charge you 2 or 3 percent of any balance transfer amount that you make. Some will charge you that 2 or 3 percent up to a certain amount, say a maximum of $50. Either way, those are pretty hefty fees.

You should also know when the promotional period expires on any balance transfer offer. If it's six months, then you should plan to pay off the balance before that time in order to reap the full benefits of that 0 percent offer you received.

Another problem with balance transfers has to do with the payment hierarchy tied to these offers. Although the amount of money you transfer from one card to another will qualify for the low rate that's offered, if you make other charges on the new card, those new charges typically carry a higher rate—not the promotional, teaser rate. When you make your regular monthly payments, you may think that those payments are going to pay off your new charges, the ones that have, say, a 15 percent interest rate. But in reality, the credit card company is applying your payments to the older balance first (i.e., the transferred balance). So any new charges you make continue to accrue interest at a higher interest rate, and it ultimately takes you longer and costs you more money to pay off your entire balance in full.

Needless to say if six months roll around and you haven't paid off the balance transfer amount, then that debt also jumps from the teaser rate to the standard, higher interest rate.

5. Avoid implementing balance transfers too frequently. Limit any balance transfers to one a year—certainly no more than two within an 18-month time period. The reason for this is that you don't want to have a whole bunch of hard inquiries and new applications for credit on your credit file. That can drag down your FICO score.

HOW "INQUIRIES" AND NEW CREDIT APPLICATIONS AFFECT YOUR CREDIT RATING

Let's do a quick, one minute test assessing your knowledge about how various things affect your credit rating. Are the following statements true or false?

- Every time you apply for credit, that application worsens your credit score.
- You shouldn't check your credit too frequently because that can hurt your FICO credit score.
- Those inquiries on your credit report from lenders who wanted to make you credit card offers are lowering your credit score.

Believe it or not, they're all false!

Here's what you need to know about how inquiries of all different kinds impact your credit profile. There are two types of inquiries that are made on your credit report: soft inquires and hard inquiries. Anytime you apply for credit—by seeking a credit card, a mortgage, or an auto loan, for example—that is called a hard inquiry. A soft inquiry occurs any time you want to look up your own credit report. Soft inquires do not hurt your credit FICO score at all. As a consumer, you have the right to check your credit file and get your FICO score as many times as you want and those inquiries won't negatively affect your credit standing one bit.

Likewise, when banks and other institutions want to determine to what individuals they will extend credit offers, they will routinely examine thousands of credit files, if not hundreds of thousands, before deciding to whom they will send various offers. These banks look at your credit history, along with scores of other people's credit reports, and the result is an inquiry on your credit report. But this is a soft inquiry, and it does nothing to impact your FICO score, because you did not ask them for credit. They were simply scouring the universe to find individuals who fit a predetermined credit profile for some new offer they were trying to make.

On the other hand, if you apply for credit, even an increase of your credit limit, or perhaps a business loan, then a financial institution will likely pull your credit report. This is considered a hard inquiry and it can—but not necessarily will—impact your FICO score.

How will you know if an inquiry will affect your FICO score? The answer lies in how many hard inquiries you've had in a given time frame. If you can limit your hard inquiries and applications for new credit accounts to no more than one (maybe two at the maximum) every 12 to 18 months maximum, that won't hurt your FICO score much at all, perhaps just a few points. With more inquiries than that, you can expect your FICO score to begin declining to a greater degree. Some experts suggest that for each inquiry beyond one or two inquiries a year, your credit score will fall anywhere from 6 to 12 points. So be careful about how many hard inquiries you have on your credit file by only applying for credit when it's absolutely necessary.

BUILDING A CREDIT RATING WITHOUT TAKING ON NEW DEBTS

To improve your credit standing, you must first know how the credit reporting system works. The Big Three credit-reporting agencies are Equifax, Experian, and TransUnion. These are the giants of the credit-reporting world, although there are actually hundreds of credit bureaus out there.

The old, conventional wisdom was that a big part of improving your credit was amassing new debt (i.e., getting a credit card, mortgage, or auto loan)and then paying those bills on time. Nowadays, we recognize that there are a number of other strategies you can utilize to bolster your credit record, without having to go into debt to do so.

Make Sure Your Credit Report Is Accurate

1. Begin by getting your credit report from one of the cred-it-reporting agencies. Even better, you can get both your credit report and FICO credit score from Fair Isaac (*www. myfico.com*), creator of the FICO credit scores that are used by most lenders in this country.

    The amount of data that they collect on the aver-age consumer is mind-boggling: everything about any student loans you've ever had, information about where you've been employed, listings about your current or pre-vious addresses, data about mortgages, credit cards, or auto loans you've taken out, and so on. Now what do you think would happen if one of these Big Three agencies had some erroneous information about you? Needless to say, it could create a nightmare for you. Not only a paper-work nightmare, not only a financial nightmare, but often times, consumers have to put in a lot of work and time to fix some errors in their credits report.

    Unfortunately, mistakes of all kinds occur in credit re-ports all too often. The Consumer Federation of America and a number of other consumer groups estimate that 70 percent of all credit reports have mistakes in them. If you find that your credit report contains errors, it definitely behooves you to fix those mistakes as soon as possible. This is one way in which you improve your credit rating without taking on new debt.

2. Examine the report for errors. Let's say you find that there is an error in one or more of them. It may be some-thing like an account listed that is not yours, or a debt that shows up belonging to John James Sr., and you are John James Jr., or maybe your name is spelled wrong, your address is not listed, or your employer is omitted. All of these errors or omissions are very important when it comes to your credit file.

3. Put it in writing. Your next step is to write directly to the three credit reporting bureaus and let them know about the mistakes. The errors or omitted information I just described often tend to be things that can be easily remedied.

   Typically, they will take about 30 days to get this kind of information fixed or updated. Some people, however, fail to write to Experian, TransUnion, or Equifax, and let them know about things they perceive as minor—such as a name that was spelled wrong, or information that is omitted from their file. Whether you realize it or not, that kind of thing could actually cost you money.

   When you go to get a loan, lenders like to see stability. So if your most recent place of employment is omitted, or if your current address is not listed properly on your credit report, your credit file may show old, outdated information. Gaps in your listed employment or pertaining to your place of residence may make you appear unstable, or as if you've been hopping around a lot—either from place to place or job to job. That's not a good image to project for someone who's trying to show that he or she is a creditworthy consumer. So, you certainly want to make sure that all relevant, up-to-date information is adequately reflected in your credit file.

4. Go to the source. If, however, you find that you have a dispute over something that is related to one of the credit card accounts or any other account that is profiled in your credit report, the first step is always to go directly to the source of information. Assume you saw a listing for one of your credit cards and the bank that issued the card has indicated that you had a 30-day late payment. If you are absolutely certain that you were not late on your payment, you should contact that bank right away.

   It's always better to resolve issues like these with the entity that supplied the credit bureau with the information. If you can address a problem with the source of information, that erroneous information will be more quickly taken off your credit report—and will likely remain off. Should you go directly to the credit reporting bureau to try to get erroneous information like that removed, they may take it off because they have 30 days, by law, to investigate your claims. So they usually go to your creditor, in this case the bank, and inquire about the alleged late payment. If the bank does not respond in a timely manner, or if the information in question is not able to be verified, then by law that has to be taken off of your credit report.

Unfortunately, what also happens is that sometimes when information has been taken off a credit report by the credit bureau, it will reappear later. It might be 60 days, six months, or three years later. But that negative, erroneous information has a way of popping up again unless you get the problem fixed with the bank that is the original supplier of that information to the credit bureaus.

There are other cases in which you want to write to the creditors, not the credit bureaus. These include situations where your credit report notes that you have a balance, but you paid that balance. Some accounts maybe duplicated or listed in different ways. You don't want the same account listed multiple times (unless it's showing a consolidated balance or a loan payoff); those multiple accounts can make it look as if you are overextended from a credit standpoint.

In summary, any errors you find in your credit report that are descriptive in nature—referencing where you live or work, your personal information, such as the spelling of your name or your Social Security number—those are cases where you write directly to the credit bureaus. For anything specifically account-related, if you are contesting the information in your credit file, go right to the source of the information. Try to work it out with them initially, and then get them to update the information with all three credit reporting agencies. Get a letter in writing that they have in fact done so. I suggest that if you have a conversation with a bank, credit card company, or lender of any type in which the outcome is that they are supposed to update your credit report, make sure you follow up that conversation in writing. Mail a letter summarizing your conversation, and send that letter certified, return receipt requested through the U.S. Postal Service. Lastly, follow up with the Big Three credit bureaus in 60 to 90 days to make sure that your accounts were, in fact, updated and any misinformation was fixed as agreed.

Show a Track Record

If you want to build up your credit report without taking on new debts, there's a way to do it that can be especially advantageous for students, recent college grads, and others looking to build or re-establish their credit. The alternative is to use a service like Payment Reporting Builds Credit (*www.prbc.com*). This organization lets you use any recurring bills, like rent or utility payments, as the basis for showing a stable credit history and building credit. In other words, you need not apply for credit, and take on debt, in order to build credit. You can just show your track record of paying certain obligations on time, and lenders can use this nontraditional information as an indication of how reliable and creditworthy you are.

The experts at Fair Isaac are also launching their own alternative scoring system, called a FICO Expansion score, for individuals with nontraditional credit data. Like the original FICO credit risk score, the FICO Expansion score rank-orders consumers by the likelihood that they will become severely delinquent (90 days or more past-due on a credit account) in the 24 months following scoring.

The universe of people without traditional credit files is enormous. Of the 215 million credit-eligible adults in the United States, some 50 million people don't have traditional credit scores, according to Fair Isaac. These include immigrants, young adults, recently divorced or widowed individuals, and members of ethnic groups that typically don't use credit. The FICO Expansion score ranges from 300 to 850, and like the classic score, the higher your score, the better a lending risk you are.

If you don't have a traditional credit file or would like to obtain your FICO Expansion score, it will soon be available at *www.myfico. com*. You can also call Fair Isaac at 1-866-838-3427 for information about your FICO Expansion score.

SNEAKY TRICKS SOME CREDIT CARD COMPANIES PLAY

Part of being a wise consumer when it comes to managing credit is knowing what games some credit card companies play that can wind up costing you money. If you are a smart consumer, part of what you have to do is to watch out for different tricks or gimmicks of the credit card industry. Frankly, these tricks they use are all very legal, but I think some of them represent questionable practices at best in terms of what credit card companies are doing which (intentionally or otherwise) trips up consumers really puts your credit health in jeopardy.

Universal Default

If you check the fine print in your credit card statements, you will find that many credit card companies tell you that they have the right the check your credit report periodically, and you'll see from your credit file that they do, in fact, examine your credit status from time to time. You may be a Visa cardholder of, say, five years, or perhaps you've had that American Express for ten years, or maybe that MasterCard or Discover Card in your wallet has been there since you can remember. Well, the reality is that in today's credit environment, these companies are all engaging in very highly sophisticated forms of risk management. These are their words, not mine: risk management.

They are essentially trying to weed out potential customers that they think might not be as good a credit risk. So part of what they do is to constantly watch, monitor, and scrutinize your spending patterns and your credit file. And what do you think happens when they are constantly watching and looking at your credit status? Any little thing that you do that falls outside of the bounds of accepted behavior—such as paying a bill late—subjects you to something called universal default. Universal default simply means that if you default on one loan of any sort, you are considered to have universally defaulted on all your debts.

What this means, in practice, is that if you're a long-standing customer of Bank XYZ, and you've faithfully paid your bills on time to that bank, but then you skip your auto loan payment for whatever reason, or you are 30 days late on another credit card payment, well, all of a sudden even your card that is in good standing with Bank XYZ is threatened. With universal default, Bank XYZ can raise your interest rate on that card to a default rate—typically around 25 percent or so—just because you've been late paying another creditor. Sounds unfair, right? Well, again, it's perfectly legal—unfortunately.

The Billing Cycle

Beyond universal default, you should know about your credit card's billing cycle. Be cautious with any cards using the double billing cycle, because that determines when it is that you are going to pay interest on the things that you purchased. You might think that you are going to pay interest after you get the bill or after a set number of days. But often, that is not the case. You might start getting charged for interest the day that you make the purchase.

The grace period on a lot of credit agreements are shrinking dramatically too. Remember the old days, when you used to have 30 days after you shopped and made a charge to mail in your payment? Or in some cases, after you got the statement in the mail, you had X number of weeks to turn it around and get that payment in to your creditor? Well, increasingly most banks and credit card issuers are using grace periods that have shrunk from 30 days to 25 and now to the 20-day mark. So by the time your closing date occurs, it's possible that you might have charged something on the 15th, and your billing cycle might end on the 25th, and from that point on the credit card company will send you the bill. The net result is that from the date that bill is sent, you'll effectively have about ten days (including mail time) to get your payment in on time to your creditor. Look on the back of your credit card agreement and find out what the grace period is for each of the cards you carry.

Mail Madness Trap

The mail madness trap is a no-win situation that a lot of other consumers find themselves subjected to with credit card companies. This trap has to do with you getting your payment in on time when you are sending it through the mail. Some credit card companies have fine print notices that state that they can legally count your credit card payment as having been received many days after it actually arrived at the company. How is this possible?

Well, the credit card issuers give you a notice that basically says you have to use their envelopes or else risk late payments and other penalties. Let's say you turned in your credit card payment on the fifth, the date when it was due. But let's also say that you just used a plain white envelope to mail your check, and you didn't send that payment inside the self addressed, preprinted envelope that the company provided—to route it to their payment processing center or wherever they want checks sent. Well, legally, just because you didn't use what they deem to be the proper envelope, your payment will not be considered to have been received in their office for another three to five days after the time that they actually received it.

I know it sounds crazy! But you actually passively agree to this—and other terms spelled out in your credit card agreement—when you accept the card and then use it without contesting these conditions. What do you think happens to consumers who fall into this mail madness trap? Untold thousands of people probably make their payments on time, but just because they didn't use the company-dictated envelope, they get slammed with late payments.

For all you know your payment sits around the mailroom for a day or two before it ever gets processed.

And here's where things get even trickier. Most credit card companies will specify not only the date by which your payment must be received, but also the time by which it is due on that date. For instance, your payment due on the fifth might have to be processed in their office by noon. Now let's say the mail gets delivered every day at 2 PM—bam! You get hit with a late fee if you get your payment in on that day. Even if they mail gets delivered by 10 AM daily you still might be subjected to potential late fees, if, for instance, the mail guy doesn't even sort the mail and bring it to the appropriate department until sometime past that noon deadline.

Late fees are huge these days. They represent a very big profit center for credit card companies, in the tens of billions of dollars. In terms of fee income, this is one of the ways that consumers get tripped up and credit card companies get rich. So take care to get your payments in well before the printed due date and time shown on your credit card statement.

Fees and Freebies

Sure a credit card company might offer you certain "freebies" in that stack of paperwork that you are getting along with your statement. Sure, they might say you can do a balance transfer or take advantage of a new credit card offer with a lower interest rate. But in reality there is always a catch.

Remember that saying: if something sounds too good to be true, it usually is? This applies in spades when you're dealing with many credit card issuers. Remember those balance transfer fees we discussed? That's an area where you really have to be careful. You're not getting free money when you use one of those checks to shift debt from one credit card to another. So you have to be aware of the fees and other provisions tied to balance transfer deals; the terms of which are noted in the fine print.

Binding Arbitration

If some of these rules and terms from credit card companies irk you, perhaps nothing will get you as upset as binding arbitration. This, in my opinion, is something that should be outrageous to consumers nationwide. In fact, there is a movement going on right now from a number of consumers groups to outlaw binding arbitration in a number of areas—not just with credit card agreements.

In a nutshell, binding arbitration means that you agree to go to a form of arbitration where you give up your right to sue or to pursue a remedy in court if there is some kind of major dispute that you have with your credit company. Why is this important? Well, what if a credit company does something egregious that is harmful not only to you individually, but to tens of thousand of consumers or possibly millions of people? What if they flat out engage in deceptive advertising or they constantly promise one thing to draw you in as a customer, and then try to hold you to a whole new set or terms or they fail to stick to their originally promised agreement? A number of companies have been accused of these very tactics, and they've had to pay fines and penalties, or make settlements to get out of those problems.

With binding arbitration, though, the consumer's hands are bound. It limits our ability to seek redress because you do not have the recourse to go into court to settle a dispute and to have a judge or a jury to hear your side of the problem. Unfortunately, binding arbitration clauses are increasingly being found in a number of areas affecting consumers and investors, including brokerage account agreements and agreements you may have with health care providers.

Most consumer advocates agree that binding arbitration clauses are usually not in the public's best interests. These can be particularly onerous for credit card users. You want to retain the right, if necessary, to go to court if something is done by a creditor that it is illegal or unfair.

PREVENT IDENTITY THEFT FROM RUINING YOUR CREDIT

You can't open the paper or look on the news without learning about how yet another criminal has stolen the identity of some unsuspecting victim. Identity theft occurs when a person misappropriates your personal information, like your Social Security number or your driver's license, and then uses that data for his or her own financial gain. For example, if thieves get hold of your Social Security number, they might open up a number of credit card accounts without your knowledge or consent. That is fraud.

The Federal Trade Commission says that this type of fraud accounts for 60 percent of all the complaints of it receives. Clearly identity theft is a huge problem. In fact, identity theft is the fastest-growing white collar crime in the country.

Here are some ideas about what you can do to thwart an identity thief:

1. Never give out your Social Security number, or only do so when it is absolutely necessary. If you are in a store or doing business with someone who requests your Social

Security number, ask them if you can give them a substitute number, like your driver's license. Resist giving out your Social Security number because it represents the keys to the kingdom for an identity thief.

2. Do not ever—under any circumstances—give out your personal information over the phone or the Internet to someone who has contacted you unsolicited. If it is a legitimate company, tell the representative that you will not give out this information due to the threat of identify theft. Ask for their 800 number so you can call back, or request written material by mail that you can evaluate it on your own time. You never know who could be calling on the other end of the phone, no matter how professional or legitimate they may sound.

3. Shred sensitive information. Sensitive information is anything from free credit offers to credit card bills—anything that might have your identifying information or your credit numbers on there. Some thieves engage in what is called dumpster diving. In other words, they get your information right out of the trash. Do not make it easy for them to do this.

4. Keep your wallet in a secure place. If you are at work, make sure you keep your wallet, purse, or whatever you use to carry money and credit cards in a locked drawer. Believe it or not, the workplace is one of the main places where identity theft occurs.

5. Keep an eye on your credit report. At the very least you should be checking your credit file once a year. You can now get your credit report free of charge, thanks to a new federal law, from all three credit reporting agencies: TransUnion, Equifax, and Experian. All you have to do is log on to *www.annualcreditreport.com* to take a look at what's in your credit file.

6. Don't carry your credit cards with you unnecessarily. If

you get robbed, or a thief steals your purse at the movies, at least they'll only get your bag, but not all of your credit information.

7. Purchase identity theft insurance. This insurance reimburses your for your out of pocket expenses like time lost on the job, mailing costs, and even sometimes the expense of having a lawyer to clean up the mess that an identity thief has created. There are a number of companies that offer identity theft insurance, such as American Express, American International Group (AIG), Farmer's, and Traveler's Insurance.

If you are victimized by identity theft—and it does affect as many as 10 million Americans each year—make sure you notify all the credit bureaus immediately. They can put an alert on your credit file and that will freeze it for the time being so that no one else that can open up unauthorized accounts without your permission.

You should also contact your local police department. Report what happened, and do not be shy about it at all because it could be the case that somebody in your general vicinity or your region is victimizing other people as well. Your tips might help the local police department crack the case.

Finally, notify the Federal Trade Commission (*www.fcc.gov*). There is also a fabulous resource center in San Diego called the Identity Theft Resource Center (*www.idtheftcenter.org*).

It's my sincere hope that you never find yourself subjected to the very awful affects of identity thief. But if you do, at least you'll know some steps to take and how to handle yourself accordingly.

CREDIT TIPS FOR COUPLES

Let me conclude this chapter by offering some tips for couples who are merging financial lives and managing credit accounts together. As with most areas in a relationship where compromise is necessary, the same thing will be true of your finances. So you'll have to collectively decide a multitude of things concerning money.

You may decide whether to buy a house together, whether to pay off one party's debts first, whether or not to have a baby, or when one person in the relationship can quit his or her job to start a business. All of these conversations have one central thread: money is involved. And if you're in a relationship, I assume you don't make unilateral decisions about all of these weighty topics.

You'll probably also want to decide whether to have separate accounts. Personally, I think it's advisable to have three separate accounts: his, hers, and ours. Couples can pay joint bills out of the ours account, which is really used to cover household expenses and other collective bills. People with their own accounts (whether checking accounts or savings accounts) also enjoy three benefits:

1. They get the freedom of spending, within reason, on the things they want. The strategy here is to put money into the joint account to fund all the household bills. And then each party can take an agreed-upon amount that's left over and put money into his or her own personal account. With the funds from such accounts, each party is free to spend on whatever he or she choose. No one has to ask for "permission" or get the other person's OK on spending choices.

2. Another plus of having a separate account is that it teaches each person financial independence. You're solely responsible for balancing your own checkbook, or keeping up with the money in your savings account, and you don't abdicate that responsibility to your partner.

3. Lastly, having three separate accounts is just a practical method of dealing with family finances for many couples— one that eliminates money battles and helps couples work together in a more cohesive, harmonious fashion.

Another frequent question I get is whether someone with good credit should put off marrying someone with bad credit until the person with bad credit cleans up his or her act. Here's my advice on that scenario. If you really want to get married, go ahead and do so without worries about your fiancé's bad credit, because the truth of the matter is that each individual's credit file and credit scores are maintained separately. Credit files do not get merged, even when two people marry. If a man with good credit is engaged to a woman with bad credit and large bills, the obligations that she had in the past are her legal and financial responsibility; not his.

A word of warning however: If, after you get married, the two of you open up credit card accounts together or you get loans (e.g., mortgages, car notes, etc.) jointly, then you both would be responsible for paying off those debts. Also, information about those loans will be listed (separately) in each of your credit files. Even if you should later divorce, if joint accounts were involved, you'd both be on the hook to pay back those debts.

In the meantime, for those who are worried about property you may own before marriage, you can keep the house in your name, and then later (once your spouse cleans up his or her credit and is financially stable), you can add his or her name to the mortgage if you want to go that route. The overall effort should be to work together as a team. That's the best way to build a strong financial future—and you can do it faster with two people pulling in the same direction, as opposed to working at odds with each other.

AFTERWORD: A CALL TO ACTION

We all should care about the exploding student debt problem in America because the mushrooming student loan crisis affects our society in many ways. If lawyers, healthcare professionals, and indebted liberal arts majors can't afford to perform public interest work-such as volunteering, mentoring, and providing free or low-cost services to those in inner cities-then a range of social ills is likely to befall these short-changed members of society.

We all also play a price in the global marketplace, because if debt-laden graduates can't further their education or upgrade their skills that weakens the competitiveness of the American workforce. The question therefore, is quite a simple one: What can be done to eliminate or reduce the problem of enormous student loan in America?

Cheaper Student Loans

One basic solution is to make the loans that students do get more affordable. It's a shame that some people are paying higher interest rates on their student loans than they are on their mortgages, auto loans, and even credit cards.

Bigger Grants-Fewer Loans

Increased funding support for higher education is vitally important. "We're at a 25-year low in terms of state support for education," notes Tamara Draut, Director of the Economic Opportunity Program at Demos, a New York-based policy group and think tank. "That money has to be made up somehow, and schools are making up for it by raising tuition prices." Unfortunately, Draut adds, the trend is away from need-based aid (which favors low-

and middle-income students) to merit-based aid. The type of aid students receive, therefore, is also critical.

"We absolutely need more grant-based aid," suggests Draut, who is also the author of *Strapped: Why Americas 20- and 30-Somethings Can't Get Ahead.* "In the late 1970s, a Pell Grant covered about three-fourths of the cost of a higher education. Today it covers about a third. So student are increasingly turning to loans." Pell Grants are currently capped at $4,050, a figure that Congress hasn't raised since 2003, despite escalating college costs. Effective January 1, 2007, the loan limits on federal Stafford loans were raised to $3,500 from $2,625 for freshmen, and to $4,500 from $3,500 for sophomores.

Student Loan Payments Tied to Your Individual Circumstances

One worthwhile proposal that does re-imagine the federal student loan system is the Plan for Fair Loan Payments from The Project on Student Debt. It would limit student loan payments to a reasonable percentage of income and recognize that borrowers with children have less income available for student loan payments.

According to executive director Robert Shireman, key features of the plan were incorporated into a Senate bill called "The Student Debt Relief Act," which was just proposed as of this writing. The bill would also raise the limit for Pell Grants to $5,100 for the 2007-08 academic year, with gradual increases up to a maximum of $6,300 in the 2011-12 academic year. If approved by legislators, Pell Grant awards would increase annually.

Addressing the Private Loan Issue

Private loans made to U.S. students make up the fastest-growing segment of the enormous student loan industry. According to the College Board, college students borrowed an unprecedented $17.3 billion worth of private loans in 2005-06, up a whopping 913% from a decade earlier. And while private loans used to be popular mainly with older graduate students, that's changed. Now, some 85% of private loans provided by market leader Sallie Mae now go to younger, less experienced undergrads. And the growth of these loans is alarming to many observers.

"The emergence of private student loans has created a hazardous situation where students are not getting any kind of counseling and advice about whether that loan is needed and whether that loan has good terms and conditions," says Shireman, from the Project on Student Debt. He says "95-plus % of those (private) loans are variable loans that may or may not look good at the start, but will go up if interest rates rise. They also don't have death and disability or hardship provisions that go with federal loans."

A Better Future and a More Sane Student Loan System

Making college more affordable and ideas about lending caps-which are either liked or despised, depending on whom you ask-will no doubt remain a recurring part of the debate. No matter what happens on the policy front, there are some things that parents and students can do to help themselves, and ensure a better future for up-and-coming generations of college students.

That's what *Zero Debt for College Grads* is all about. The strategies, insights and tips in this book will give you the confidence and knowledge you need to successfully pay off your student loans, properly handle your other bills, and not sacrifice your sanity or financial security in the process. Best wishes to you in all your endeavors-personally, professionally and financially!

Lynnette Khalfani, The Money Coach
http://www.themoneycoach.net

ACKNOWLEDGMENTS

Writing *Zero Debt for College Grads* has almost felt like getting another degree: lots of research and writing, a tremendous amount of hard work, some angst-filled nights—but ultimately, such an enormous feeling of accomplishment and pride in the final outcome. None of this would have been possible if it weren't for a number of very talented and helpful individuals.

To my fiancé, agent and manager, Earl Cox of Earl Cox & Associates: thanks again for another brilliant book idea. I'm so happy to extend the *Zero Debt* franchise, and with your strategic guidance, creativity, and industry knowledge, I know that we will continue to build upon this very strong series. On a personal note, Earl, you've brought so much happiness and contentment into my life. How can I ever repay you for all your love and support?

To Deborah Darrell of Cue, my media strategist: you always teach me so much about presentation, style and substance. I feel like you're one of the secret weapons in everything that I do—whether it's a TV appearance, book project or speaking engagement. My work gets better and better with you in my camp.

To the entire editorial, sales and marketing team at Kaplan: many thanks for your care and attention to this project. To Kaplan publisher Maureen McMahon: I'm grateful for your enthusiasm and long-standing desire to work with me. To my editor, Shannon Berning: my heartfelt appreciation for all your keen feedback throughout this process. You kept me squarely focused on our target audience, edited this book with great professionalism and passion, and did a first-rate job of organizing the material in ways I could never have done alone. To publicity director Yvette Romero: thanks for jumping right in to promote this book as soon as you came to Kaplan. Your responsiveness and can-do spirit has shined from day one. To production editor Julio Espin and marketing director Dino Battista, special thanks to you both for being so easy to work with and getting this book off to a great start.

Lastly, I owe a debt of gratitude to the numerous people who allowed me to interview them for this book, and to the thousands of people who've written me over the years seeking advice to wipe out their debts and achieve financial freedom. Without you, *Zero Debt for College Grads* wouldn't have meaning.

APPENDIX: ZERO DEBT CHECKLIST

After reading *Zero Debt for College Grads*, you should be able to take the following action steps to improve your personal finances. Each of the items listed below will help you to manage your current bills, pay off your student loans, or build your credit rating.

Chapter 1

❏ Write down your gross and net (after-tax) monthly income

❏ Create a realistic monthly budget, taking into account your true monthly expenses

❏ Log onto *www.myannualcreditreport.com* for free copies of your credit reports from TransUnion, Experian, and Equifax, the three primary credit reporting agencies in the U.S.

❏ Visit *www.myfico.com* to obtain your FICO credit scores from Fair Isaac, the company that creates credit scores used by the nation's top banks and financial institutions

Chapter 2

❏ Evaluate your housing costs. Are affordable options, like having a roommate, feasible?

❏ Calculate the true cost of owning your car including insurance, gas, repairs, car notes, etc.

❏ List seven ways you can cut your food, entertainment, and clothing expenses

❏ Write down two things you will do immediately to decrease your utility bills

❏ Contact your insurance company to see if you qualify for any discounts

Chapter 3

☐ Adjust your withholdings at work, using form W-4, if you receive a tax refund check

☐ Put together a list of your accomplishments; then request a raise from your boss

☐ Enroll in your 401(k) or 403(b) plan at work; or increase your retirement contributions

☐ Sell or donate clothing, household goods, and other items you no longer want or need

☐ Visit *www.missingmoney.com* or *www.unclaimed.org* to see if you are owed "free" money

Chapter 4

☐ Log onto *www.pin.ed.gov* and obtain a four-digit PIN to get information about your federal student loans

☐ Visit the National Student Loan Data System at *www.nslds.ed.gov* to get a complete listing of all your federal student loans

☐ Call the Federal Student Aid Information Center at 1-800-4-FED-AID (1-800-433-3243) to track down very old loans, or for information about your loan holder and loan history

☐ Contact your school directly, call your lender, or refer to your original promissory note for information about private loans

Chapter 5

☐ Use the online financial calculators found at *www.finaid.org/calculators* to determine your total student loan repayment amounts under four different scenarios: the standard, extended, graduated, and income contingent repayment plans

☐ Consider whether you can afford to pay an "extra" amount on your monthly student loan payments

☐ Contact your lender and request the following perks: an interest rate reduction for automatic deductions; a lowered interest rate for on-time payments; reduced or eliminated fees; cash rebates or reduced fees for good payers

☐ Obtain the Statement of Financial Status form from the Department of Education at: *www.ed.gov/offices/OSFAP/DCS/forms/fs.pic.pdf* if you are having problems making student loan payments because you have other bills that are unusually high

Chapter 6

☐ Write down the interest rates on each of your federal student loans. Now take the average interest rate and round it up to the nearest 1/8th of 1 percent in order to determine your interest rate if you consolidated your student loans

☐ Visit *www.simpletuition.com* and use their consolidation comparison tools to compare multiple financing options from a variety of lenders, and to sort consolidation loan offers by monthly payment, total cost of the loan, number of payments, fees, and annual percentage rates

☐ For assistance in finding a loan consolidation company, call 1-800-433-3243 for an FFEL lender, or contact the Direct Loan Origination Center's Consolidation Department at 1-800-557-7392

Chapter 7

☐ Contact your lender or loan servicing company to inquire about whether you qualify for a deferment if you are having trouble making payments

☐ Call your lender to request a forbearance if you cannot afford your student loans and you did not qualify for a deferment

☐ Seek help or information from the Federal Student Aid Office of the Ombudsman (online at *www.ombudsman.ed.gov*, or via telephone at 1-877-557-2575) if you have a problem or dispute with a lender that you cannot resolve

Chapter 8

☐ If you have a defaulted student loan, contact the guaranty agency, your lender, or servicer and find out who is currently holding the loan

☐ Inquire with your lender about your eligibility for loan consolidation in order to bring a past-due student loan out of default status

❒ Request information from your lender or loan servicer about how much your monthly payments would be to go through "loan rehabilitation" in order to cure a defaulted student loan

❒ To fight a wage garnishment, obtain and fill out a Financial Disclosure Statement, which is available via the Department of Education at *www. ed.gov/offices/OSFAP/DCS/forms/fs.pdf*.

Chapter 9

❒ Investigate whether you qualify for any loan cancellation or discharges

❒ Look into loan forgiveness programs you may be eligible for based on your job or community-based work/volunteering you would be willing to undertake

❒ Request that your employer pay off all or a portion of your student loans as a retention tool, in exchange for your commitment to remain employed at your place of business

❒ Visit the website of the U.S. Office of Personnel Management (*www.opm. gov*) to read up on the federal Student Loan Repayment Program and learn more about government work that could qualify you to have $60,000 worth of student loans paid off on your behalf. Consider whether you would take a government job in order to be eligible for this benefit.

Chapter 10

❒ Create a list of all your credit card debts. Write down the names of your creditors, your account numbers, balances due, interest rates, and minimum monthly payments

❒ Pick a debt payoff strategy based on what bothers you most about your credit card debt: high interest rates, high dollar balances, or too many credit card accounts

❒ Call each one of your creditors and request lower interest rates on all your credit cards

❒ Contact your credit card companies to negotiate the removal of late payment penalties, annual charges, or over-the-limit fees

❒ To settle past-due obligations, call your old creditors and propose a settlement - for pennies on the dollar. Insist that any payments you send to clear up your account be made in exchange for all negative information being eliminated from your credit files. Send written letters certified mail, return receipt requested to confirm the details of your settlements

❏ Request a change in your credit card due dates if all your bills come due around the same time of the month causing you to routinely experience a cash crunch

Chapter 11

❏ Evaluate your credit files to check for any mistakes or incomplete information

❏ Call your creditors, or write directly to the credit bureaus, to get errors in your credit reports fixed

❏ Resist the urge to close out old credit card accounts or transfer balances the wrong way

❏ Review your credit card statements to determine all the terms of your card agreements

❏ Set your credit card payments up on automatic payment plans to ensure your bills are paid on time each month

❏ Shred sensitive financial documents, avoid giving out your social security number, and take unnecessary credit cards out of your wallet to prevent identity theft

❏ Pat yourself on the back for reading *Zero Debt for College Grads*, taking control of your finances, and getting on the road to financial freedom!

RESOURCES

Auto Refinancing or Information Sites
Capital One Auto Finance
www.capitaloneauto.com
Kelley Blue Book
www.kbb.com
Loans at E-loan
www.eloan.com
Vehicle History Reports
www.carfacts.com

College Lenders and Student Loan Information Providers
Citibank
www.citibank.com
My Rich Uncle Student Loans
www.myrichuncle.com
National Student Clearinghouse
www.studentclearinghouse.org
Sallie Mae - Private Student Loans, Stafford, PLUS, Student Loan Consolidation
www.salliemae.com
Simple Tuition
www.simpletuition.com
Student Aid Lending
www.studentaidlending.com
The Smart Student Guide to Financial Aid
www.finaid.org

Credit Information Sites
Annual Credit Report
www.annualcreditreport.com
Equifax
www.equifax.com
Experian
www.experian.com
Identity Theft Resource Center
www.idtheftcenter.org
Fair Isaac Corporation
www.myfico.com
Federal Trade Commission
www.ftc.gov
Payment Reporting Builds Credit
www.prbc.com
TransUnion
www.transunion.com

Department of Education Resources
Direct Consolidation Loans
www.loanconsolidation.ed.gov

Federal Student Aid Gateway
www.federalstudentaid.ed.gov
Federal Student Aid PIN
www.pin.ed.gov
FSA Ombudsman Home Page
www.ombudsman.ed.gov
National Student Loan Data System for Students
www.nslds.ed.gov

Financial Aid/College Funding Resources
Free Application for Federal Student Aid
www.fafsa.ed.gov
National Association of Student Financial Aid Administrators
www.nasfaa.org
Saving for College (529 Plans)
www.savingforcollege.com
Upromise
www.upromise.com

Other Government Resources for Student Loan Info
Federal Citizen Information Center
www.pueblo.gsa.gov
U.S. Office of Personnel Management
www.opm.gov

Personal Finance Help and Financial Literacy Resources
Lynnette Khalfani, The Money Coach
www.themoneycoach.net
Money Savvy Generation
www.moneysavvygeneration.com

Professional Organizations Lobbying for Student Loan Reform
American Bar Association
www.abanet.org
American Federation of Teachers
www.aft.org
Equal Justice Works
www.equaljusticeworks.org

Public Service Groups for Loan Cancellation/Forgiveness
Americorps
www.americorps.org

Indian Health Service
    www.ihs.gov
NIH Loan Repayment Program
    www.lrp.nih.gov
Office of Statewide Health Planning and
    Development
    www.oshpd.ca.gov
Volunteers in Service to America
    www.friendsofvista.org

Student Loan Advocacy Groups
Demos
    www.demos.org
Project on Student Debt
    www.projectonstudentdebt.org
U.S. Public Interest Research Group
    www.uspirg.org

Unclaimed Money/Property
Missing Money Free Search for Unclaimed
    Property
    www.missingmoney.com
National Association of Unclaimed Property
    Administrators
    www.unclaimed.org
National Unclaimed Property Network
    www.nupn.com

INDEX

ABOUT THE AUTHOR

Lynnette Khalfani, The Money Coach, is a personal finance expert and the author of *The Money Coach's Guide to Your First Million, Investing Success: How To Conquer 30 Costly Mistakes & Multiply Your Wealth!* and the *New York Times* bestseller *Zero Debt: The Ultimate Guide to Financial Freedom.*

As an award-winning financial news journalist, Lynnette worked for nearly a decade as a Dow Jones Newswires reporter and a Wall Street Journal reporter for CNBC. She is a two-time winner of the Dow Jones International Newswires Award. She currently contributes personal finance content to SmartMoney.com, Gather.com, Black Enterprise, and Bee, a national women's magazine.

Lynnette has interviewed thousands of financial experts, and personally paid off more than $100,000 in credit card debt and nearly $40,000 worth of student loans. Now she shares the secrets to wealth with audiences nationwide, using insights based not just on her professional knowledge, but also on first-hand experience.

Lynnette is a frequent guest on national TV and radio programs, and has been featured in the *New York Times, USA Today, Redbook, Essence,* and on *The Oprah Winfrey Show, Dr. Phil, The Tyra Banks Show, The Rachael Ray Show, Tavis Smiley,* as well as the Emmy award-winning reality program "Starting Over."

When she's not chasing after her three young kids, Lynnette is developing two television projects, based around her books Zero Debt and The Money Coach's Guide to Your First Million. She conducts financial workshops and is also presently a Money Coach for AOL.

To learn about Lynnette's "Financial Boot Camp," her financial coaching services, or to sign up for her free personal finance newsletter, please visit Lynnette's website at *http://www.TheMoneyCoach.net.*